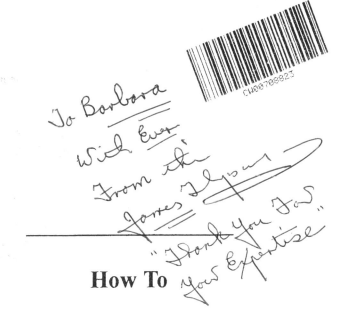

To Barbara
With Ever
From th
James Thyou
"Thank You For
Your Expertise"

How To

BOUNCE THROUGH LIFE

Acknowledgments:

To Doreen Thompson for making order out of chaos; not forgetting
John Harrison of Portknockie, Lena Cowie of Buckie and
Gillian Russell of Aberdeen.

First Published in 1996
by
Ty Coch Publishing,
Fron Park Road,
HOLYWELL, Flintshire CH8 7UY

Copyright ©James Thompson 1996

All rights reserved

ISBN 0 9523022 1 7

Other books by the same author:
Cast out of the ark
Reflections of a spiritual tramp
Praise for creatures great and small
(Further enquiries from Ty Coch Publishing at the address above)

Printed by the Delyn Press, Holywell, Flintshire, with typesetting by
R.H.Williams, Brynford, and binding by Thomas Loughlin Ltd. Liverpool
for Ty Coch Publishing.

Dedication:

**To My First Born,
Professor Dr. David Robert Thompson,
Fellow of the Royal College of Nursing,**
who has no need of such a book!

also

Rev. Dr. Bill Curtis and his
National Association of Clergy Hypnotherapists,
whom I've had the honour of addressing

&

Evangelist Derick Bingham,
who radiates the Christ he proclaims

CONTENTS

INTRODUCTION

More and more folk are turning towards alternative therapies in quest of healing, and this includes therapy for the mind. We're living in an era of vast expanse within the world of complementary medicine; and, though most turn to it when allopathy has failed them, the successes are **still** most encouraging. The causes for seeking such therapies are quite varied but three factors stand out as important and relevant: *Firstly,* allopathy, i.e. orthodox medicine, is possibly the top supporter of our vast drug industries which have become the Nation's number one health hazard; and the diseases caused through drug side effects dispensed (iatrogenic illnesses), are deemed responsible for an ever increasing number of patients hospitalised.

Secondly, these drugs are tested upon animals and this can be dangerously disastrous as their metabolism and makeup are so different from our own; on the physical side the horrendous thalidomide tragedy is a glaring example of putting onto the market for one species what was successful in another!

Thirdly, but by no means least, those who believe in the principle of moral laws, even if not in The Good Shepherd Himself, are finding it increasingly difficult to condone a system whose basic research for furthering human health on the physical and mental plain is via immoral means. Vivisection is responsible for one animal every six seconds dying within a British laboratory, and most of them die after much suffering. Vivisection has an appalling image as even the most sane and balanced of animal welfare societies the R.S.P.C.A. would forcefully affirm. Certainly, for the Christian **at least**, the justification offered for torturing a vast part of the Creation for the purpose of perpetuating the life style of the 'guardian!' species, must be open to very serious questioning. "No ultimate good can come from any evil deed - mark my words!" was the warning a Godly mother gave to her children. Yes, to many, Christians and otherwise, the sowing and reaping process (*Hosea 8:7 and Galations 6:7*) can no more be confined to one species than it could to one race. The Conservationist, with even greater insight, includes the inanimate creation as well.

Much of the complementary therapy, though considered young, is actually the oldest of medications for man's tripartite being: body, mind and spirit; holistically, modern man is beginning to appreciate their interplay in the quest for wholeness and lack of disease. The present drug possessed and symptom alleviating medical world is of comparatively modern origin within the history of mankind. It largely originated with Paracelsus in the sixteenth century. Yet, even **he** was persecuted and driven from city to city because he wisely stated that imagination and faith could cause and remove disease. The system received a further boost under Claude Bernard, father of vivisection, within the nineteenth century. He has been called The Father of Modern Medicine.

Way back amongst the ancients, however, within the land of the Bible and outside of it, the practice of positive suggestion for the mind (*Romans 12:2*) and herbalism for the body (*Psalm 104:14*) flourished; and none used the former more than the Physician from Galilee. And as for the only operation recorded in Scripture (*Genesis 2:21*) one might be excused for associating it with the Almighty's use of hypnosis, but hardly with that of gas. It need only be added that while two dentists in the States, Wells and Norton, were discovering chemical anasthesia, renowned medical men, such as Esdaile in India

and Elliotson in Britain, were performing very many highly successful major operations using hypnosis. This had necessitated them
mastering the art which had largely and indirectly evolved from two
clerics on the Continent, Hehl and Gassner. Patience was needed to
win the rapport of their patients to bring about a somnambulistic
state. Such factors were often very time consuming and only a few
acquired the necessary skills required. Consequently, once chemical
anasthesia was on the market it speedily won the day. Alas, not
without its serious annual toll of consequences down the decades.

Many alternative methods of therapy have been criticized by
opponents as little better than placebos. The fact is, however, that
nothing has as much placebo effect as a treatment or prescription
handed out by the high priests of an awed medical establishment.
Proof of the usefulness of any therapy for mind or body is in its
results; and, indeed, results within the world of alternative medicine
are reflected not only in humans who are suggestible but also via the
increasing sales of homeopathic remedies for veterinary purposes.

It is the writer's opinion that this recent surge for alternative
health guides, and the enactment of humane and caring life styles, is
partially the fulfilling of prophesies long overdue (*Romans 8: 19-22*)
in which a redeemed creation, positive and vibrant, will partake of
the leaves of the trees for the healing of the nations (*Revelation 22:2*)
and, when the Messiah arrives, will share mutual peace with the rest
of Creation (*Isaiah 11: 6 - 9*), a concept as far removed from an
Aquarian new age - with its practitioners in the occult - as is their
earth's goddess Gaya from Heaven's one and only God Jehovah!

Complementary medicine, however, bridges many barriers
and, as with conventional medicine, it embraces those of all Faiths
and none. Though its methods to heal are extremely varied, there is
a tolerance between its therapies and healers which - though far from
common amongst many Christians today - was so marked in the
Galilean Himself. (*Luke 9: 49 - 50*).

Jesus also used various means by which to heal. Yet they all worked! If there was any exception it was simply due to an obstinate spirit of unbelief on the part of the patient. There is still a state of mind which is able to remove mountains (*Matthew 17:20*). This publication, written for Christian and Non Christian alike, is confined to developing it. You'll certainly not find hints on herbs, homeopathy, acupressure or acupuncture in this volume; but, if you have faith as small as a grain of mustard seed it will enable you, in an easily readable way to cast mountains away from before your very path, or to walk unscathed right through them.

Happy reading!

James Thompson

(N.B. References from The Bible are simply added for any who may wish to refer to them as an extended form of study from this book.)

CHAPTER I

YOUR LIFE CAN BE TRANSFORMED

That you have taken the trouble to pick up this book implies that you are far from satisfied with life as it is. Or, even if you are mildly satisfied, then you are anxious to begin living life on a higher dimension. You may, indeed, feel that the title of this publication is too happy to contemplate. It may be that you consider yourself to be living quite a mediocre existence. You could never visualise the lights and zest of living which are so characteristic of the lives of other folk as being applicable to yourself. Well, this publication is written specifically with people like yourself in mind: the dreary worker in the office, the jaded shop assistant behind the counter; the fellow in the factory; the student in the classroom; yes, and the teacher at her desk. Indeed, far from least, that wonderful creation so often taken for granted: the housewife and mother in despondency, if not in confusion, amid her hectic household and family chores; and O! let us never forget that ever mounting multitude of unemployed!

Indeed, I do not limit my words to the above, for most of my time in the past professionally, has been centred round hospitals. I think of those members of the caring professions ministering to the psychologically, as well as physically, sick. These folk need not be excluded. Their lives also can be rejuvenated and revolutionised. Actually, I made no apology when, as a chaplain, I told patients that Almighty God often allows us to fall on our backs so that we may look upwards to Him! Yes, I firmly believe that God often allows us to be upset for a while so that ultimately we may be set up forever!

Of course, not all who read these pages will share the writer's Christian interpretation of life, and I shall not think less of you because of that. It need only be said that, in following even the non religious side of this book you will find your daily living considerably transformed. It will prove, I have no doubt, the most helpful 'self help' publication of its kind. In fairness to yourself however, I would ask you not to discard the spiritual side of these pages too lightly. You, dear reader, can either drive through this world on two cylinders, or, what is surely more preferable, on three. It is the Christian belief that man needs a spiritual side to his being as much as a body and a mind.

Are not people in their saner moments these days beginning to realise that their living has been incomplete? Do they not feel that they've lost a quality they were meant to possess? Surely a disorientated mind swayed by bodily appetites is not enough! It would appear that, just as nature abhors a vacuum, so in this Aquarian Age a non Christian spiritual dimension is becoming quite an attraction to the masses who are fed up with the materialist outlook which has left them spiritually bankrupt. It is, however, the writer's contention that Earth goddesses, pyramids and covens are poor substitutes for spiritual birth through commitment to Christ. If the reader wishes, he may well like to read through this publication, first with scant regard to the spiritual and scriptural side, and then read it through a second time giving full attention to these - and to those scriptural passages appended.

There is a law which is as universal as it is scriptural, Hindus and Buddhists have referred to it as the law of Karma: 'What you sow, you reap'. But alas, what we sow others may equally have to reap! You and I have already reaped much of what our parents and forefathers sowed. Some have been cradled and nurtured by parents

2

who instilled into their offspring the greatest gift a parent can give to any child - SELF - CONFIDENCE. And I have put it in capitals in case you are a parent or teacher yourself. Others amongst us are reaping the fruit of the teaching of misguided parents. We are inadequate, insecure, indecisive beings. We may be adults in years but we're stinted and, up to now, have been emotionally no more than juniors.

These latter folk, crippled on the journey through life, have come into contact with me down through the years. As a chaplain and clergyman, and in more recent years in my roles as a hypnoanalyst and psychotherapist, I've met them. Yet, I have good news! The mentally and emotionally stinted can often be transformed into what might appear, to those unaccustomed to psychotherapeutic laws, to be bordering on the miraculous. By methods such as depth analysis, catharsis, reorientation, and the use of the simple common sense therapy contained in this volume, many a weary soul who once felt inadequate is now facing life courageously instead of cowardly; optimistically instead of pessimistically. Sunshine is taking the place of showers; blessing comes from bereavement (as Jesus once promised it would) (*Matthew 5:4*) and the underling and serf becomes liberated and free. And all this becomes a daily experience.

The writer knows, experientially, the truth and value of positive teaching. For example, when he was a mere eighteen-year-old, with minimum education, he was in demand as a lay preacher. At twenty-three, he had become a bona fide Baptist minister. That early success - apart from a divine calling - was due to self-confidence, the gift of a poor, widowed mother, who taught her sons to live up to the principles of Rudyard Kipling's poem, "If", as well as to assimilate, by constantly repeating, these words: 'I am the master (though **never** oppressor) of all I survey'.

Alas, that basic confidence which many young folk acquire can so often be thwarted by academic establishments where, at a subconscious level, one learns to equate 'wisdom' with the attain-

3

ment of university or college awards conferred by staff with titles and letters after their names. Indeed, so regrettably does such indoctrination take place that many young folk have had their original sense of confidence so undermined as to become emotional cripples for later life. A subconscious complex compels them to pursue one academic qualification after another in order that they may try and prove their worth to their superiors. The outcome is that these poor creatures, having eventually acquired positions of importance because of academic bits of paper, then find themselves inadequate to fulfil their allotted tasks. Once severed from an institutional background, they no longer have an elder professor to lean on. The crutch is taken away from the academically nurtured, just as it is from the dependent child of an over-possessive parent, and the poor creature is deemed hopelessly inadequate within a competitive world.

It is strange, and yet so understandable, that those 'hedged in' or 'coddled' are to be found later amongst the misfits of life, whereas often the ones who have had the most obstacles to face have overcome them. The tree protected from the winds will be of no use in the storm. It is equally of little use being able, academically speaking, to count the number of peas in a pod when one wouldn't have the foggiest notion as to how to plant them. True maturity and true education have, alas, been precious commodities sadly lacking in most of our lives. The outcome is that, owing partly to misguided, though possibly well-intentioned parents, and to a false view of what real education for living is all about, we find ourselves feeling at times far from adequate. Hence our quest to start living with vim, vigour and vitality.

The first Christian missionary to the Gentile world, St. Paul, wrote these words to the Converts at Rome: 'Be ye transformed by the renewing of your mind'. (*Romans 12:2*). That dear, old Rabbi was shrewd and wise, for that's where it all begins: with the renewal of one's mind!

4

I suggest that, first of all, you take time to read this publication when you can do so without being unduly disturbed. There is a danger of becoming so very active doing things mechanically that one fails to use one's mind properly. And this, indeed, is often a psychological mechanism used to evade thought. We see this frequently resorted to when a dear soul is newly bereft of a loved one, for one certainly cannot be doing two things at the same time on the conscious level: on this occasion fussing around doing things and also thinking of the partner of whom one is bereft. However, though this trick of the mind is helpful as a temporary crutch during reorientation after a bereavement, such is hardly the case when folk are to be found compulsively fussing over a period of years, continually wound up and with a seeming inability to stop. When such factors do occur, and indeed they certainly do, then the cause is within that part of the mind which the father of analytical psychology termed 'the unconscious' and his first pupil of renown preferred to call 'the old mind'. I refer respectively to Sigmund Freud[1] and Carl Gustav Jung[2], his dedicated Christian successor.

Find a place for daily perusal of this book where you can give your mind to analysis of yourself so that you may face the facts of your own life as objectively as humanly possible. 'Man, Know thyself', were, indeed, the words of a great philosopher, but alas, he was hardly a good psychologist. The scriptural writer knew that the mind of man was desperately deceitful (*Jeremiah 17:9*), and the old bard William Shakespeare knew too (as is so apparent from his plays) that self-deception is more real than most folk realise. Nevertheless, we need a starting point, so see to it that you use valuable time for the most valuable thing in life: the transforming of your own self. A fool neglects the body, but of far more value to you than that outward chrysalis is the life that temporarily inhabits it. You take time to

---

1. See e.g. S.Freud. Page 336 Introductory Lectures on Psycho-anbalysis (Pelican 1973)
2. See e.g. Collect Works of Jung Vol. 9, part I, Par. 502 (Routledge & Kegan Paul Ltd. (1939)

transform your appearance by going to the boutique, and what an exhilarating effect it has on your personality. It was well and truly worth it. Then who but a fool will refuse time towards the rejuvenation and transformation of that inner life, struggling to get liberated in order that it may use new-found wings: there is a butterfly within that chrysalis: a jewel within a temporary jewel box. You do right to improve the box, but you do far greater justice to yourself in exposing to view the jewel that this physical casing contains.

In closing this opening chapter, I am not unaware that there is a branch of psychology which would affirm that man is but the victim of hereditary, biological and environmental factors. I need only say that such a theory has now been discarded by any one with a worthy approach to the human psyche. The all-out behaviourist is as off beam as that branch of Christendom termed Hyper Calvinism. The latter denies free will to man and yet denounces or appraises him for the evil or good he does! The readers, whom the writer has in mind would hardly include the psychotic and institutionalised! Such folk, because of their predicament, would unfortunately hardly seek a different life to that which they now experience. But though the psychotic has no worthwhile appreciation of his condition, the neurotic frequently has, and, actually, neuroticism of a lesser degree is part of the affliction of the mass of mankind. Indeed, the desire to live a fuller life with more bounce than that already arrived at is an indictor that we're not as we would like to be. It is as healthy a factor as the discontentment of a saint who strives for a higher goal. Be assured, for ever, it is not selfishness to want to live a fuller, nobler and more meaningful life. Happiness is contagious, and so is zest. Your future joy and optimism will rub off on others. You owe it to your neighbour, as well as to yourself, that you become a ray of sunshine and not a damp cloud. YOU can begin to live a fuller and more abundant life, and what is more, you can begin today.

CHAPTER II

INTERPRETATIONS ARE GREATER THAN FACTS

Does such a statement sound ludicrous to you? Then consider the fellow who has embarked upon a long-awaited holiday and who has just arrived at his destination. The guest-house or hotel has been booked and paid for. The environment seems most congenial - except for one factor: the weather has changed from dry and sunny to windy and extremely wet. Now it so happens that the district he is in has been in great need of rain for the crops as well as the gardens. The consequence of the wet weather is that the holidaymaker is downcast and despondent, to say the least. But, at the same time, the farmers and gardeners of the district are offering thanks and feeling jubilation for the likelihood of many days of continuous rain. The holidaymaker says, with utter annoyance, 'What beastly and deplorable weather', while the gardener and farmer are elated and in ecstasy. That the weather is good or bad is but the interpretation that each individual cares to put upon outer factors. Reality affirms but a simple fact: rain; interpretation chooses to affirm it good or evil. Now it is the interpretation of facts rather than the literal fact itself which influences one's mood. Not what a thing is, but rather what we choose to associate with it, is the factor that has the power to blight or bless us.

I constantly come across folk who are in hospital, and that they are there as patients is but a fact. How they respond, however, towards temporary confinement in a hospital bed is the factor which can either make or break them. One is reminded of a ditty which even narrates confinement within an old prison cell:

'Two men looked out from prison bars
One saw mud while the other saw stars'

It was the same cell, but whereas one looked upwards and was elated, the other looked downwards and was downcast.

A fellow on his way to work eventually arrived at the bus stop. The long-awaited bus arrived and the conductor said, 'Room for only one more'. A man from the queue boarded the bus before him. Our friend fumed and raved as the bus moved away from the stop, and for the rest of the day he viewed things with hostility. Indeed, his manner was undoubtedly contagious, and soon the rest at the office were behaving in a surly if not hostile fashion towards him. When tea-time arrived, the dear fellow returned home in a brooding spirit and, consequently, his whole family began to bear the brunt of his early morning experience. In fact, there is really far more to it than that. Our mind interacts with our body, and so the character in this episode was well on the way towards a coronary brought about by stress, as well as an ulcer through too much secretion of the body's gastric juices. That such an individual was also on the way towards wrecking his family life need hardly be mentioned. Indeed, all this turmoil and restlessness had resulted from the way he had reacted to the ignorant queue-jumper and a refusal by a conductor.

Of course, basically, the fault may well have rested originally with over-indulgent parents, who had given our subject all that he had asked for when he was a child. Or, should they have refused the first time he asked, he knew that if he sulked and brooded long enough then they would eventually give in to his every whim. Indeed, he may have been predisposed to work along these lines at an early age. Consequently, he keeps up the same brooding, trusting that such conduct will still be rewarded. Alas, he finds that, in a mature adult world, such is not the case. In a sense he is not to be blamed because, although he may be advanced in years, own a lucrative business and have many subordinates to fuss round him, he is nevertheless emotionally still no more than an infant.

A maturer person at a bus stop, having undergone the same episode, might well have said: 'Ah well, that's an experience of first class rudeness; better luck next time! I'll continue doing my crossword until the next coach arrives.'

Do not think for one moment that I am disparaging bitter or unfortunate experiences. I am merely saying that the incident that happens is, of itself, a mere objective fact and that the tone and colour we add to it are ours: if we choose to affiliate it with gloom, we shall then, in all probability, experience gloom; whereas if we choose to associate an external objective fact with pleasure, then the emotion of pleasure, as a by-product, will flow into our life.

I remember how one fellow used to stand at a bus stop constantly watching the motorists pass by. The different makes of car provided quite an interest for him while he awaited the coming of the next bus. However, should one particular Escort pass his way, immediately his emotions were aroused and he seemed 'over the moon' for the rest of the day. The fact was that he had learned to associate that particular Escort with the usual occupant of the driving seat: a lady who, on seeing him, would frequently and charmingly offer him a lift! Then let us remember that what one learns to associate with a mere external phenomenon is that which may make or mar our day: the associations are greater than the facts in the influence they have over us.

That someone whom we meet makes a statement in our presence is but a fact which, in itself, is quite harmless. 'I think we are going to have plenty of rain', is such a statement. As such, it can be neither good nor bad. But what our own individual mind cares to associate with such a possibility is indeed the crucial factor; elation

9

may be produced in the mind of one and despondency in the mind of another. Indeed, the same law applies when someone says something which truly offends us: 'I think you are a cantankerous, miserable, chauvinistic pig!' Yes, such might be the utterance of one who has reached the end of her endurance in dealing with you - presuming, of course, you are such a character! Well, that's merely an example. However, the man with a skin as hard and impenetrable as a rhinoceros is not likely to fume and fret over such a statement directed against himself. He allows such insults to roll off his back as water from a duck. Yet another dear soul, of a gentle disposition, who may be the last who should be categorised via such an insult, takes the matter to heart. The man ends up in a wounded condition. Why wounded? Because he has allowed the statement to enter his being. Yet, he had no need to. The words only hurt him because he allowed them to enter.

Almost every moment of the day people are uttering a mixture of statements and many of them are far from favourable. Indeed, some of these utterances may even be connected with ourselves. However, they do not affect our emotional equilibrium to any real extent as we hardly know of them. It is the listener who pries around who sooner or later hears, or else wrongly interprets, unkind statements as being implied of himself and because of his interpretation of such private conversations he becomes paranoiac in outlook: 'Listeners hear no good of themselves!'

You see, it's all dependent upon whether we see a statement as relevant to ourselves. We can choose to dismiss it immediately or we can allow unkind or even cruel words a place within our hearts. You and I ought to hold ourselves as sentry at every opening. We need to ask ourselves, 'Shall I allow this utterance directed towards myself access within, or shall I send it on its way?' Indeed, you accept a delightful sweet into your mouth while a bitter sweet you immediately spit out, and if you'd had known the latter to be bitter you would have barred your mouth to it at the beginning. We need to affirm a similar discipline in our minds. Such mental discipline and assertiveness is as vital to our emotional sanity as physical restraint and discipline is to our bodies.

If we refuse to practice the above discipline - and practice alone will make perfect - then we will suffer immeasurably by allowing deadly arrows to penetrate us. And that they often are deadly is no mere exaggeration. Many of these arrows are poison-tipped. Once they have been allowed to penetrate the skin, then the poison begins to fester and all the poultices in the world are insufficient to stop the damage. Smoking to excess, and trying to drown one's sorrows merely makes them float to the surface. Why, even a holiday on the Riviera will never compensate for the poison you have allowed, and crazily welcomed, into your being. Let me illustrate.

A lady has a row with a neighbour and her husband has a row with his boss. Thankfully, they think, they'll be able to get away from it all as their holiday to the Canary Isles begins the next day. However, on arriving at their destination and reclining on a warm and glorious beach, they allow themselves to think of those unkind folk back in Britain. What happens? They shuffle around and inwardly fume, wondering how they might get even with those opponents back home. The result is that their blood pressure goes up and the adrenalin flows without serving any physical purpose such as fight or flight. Consequently the whole metabolism of the body is under strain, with quite unhealthy results. Of course, the results, such as heart trouble, respiratory disease and peptic ulcers, might take years to manifest. But think, nevertheless, of their present holiday: they are on a delightful beach and yet they might just as well be in their back garden for all the good it is doing them, as they are tossing and turning as they contemplate the enemy. Like victims of a sore tooth, they can appreciate nothing else because of that one nagging factor.

But let us move on. The hotel has provided for them truly wonderful meals: can they enjoy them? No, of course not. They might cram down as much food as their stomachs can hold. Yet their digestive juices are so affected as to be unable to function as they should. Who could possibly enjoy food when the stomach is churned up because of psychosomatic factors? But then the hours pass and the best is yet to be - at least such is the anticipation of both. The bedroom is done out in quite a luxurious manner; the bed itself is exotic and alluring. However, anxiety and sexual bliss are the worst bedmates, and so an inhibition in the sex drive becomes a reality: neither of them can function as adequately as they should. Possibly one cannot function at all! So they decide they must just roll over and fall into a blissful sleep. Alas, this they cannot do. Their mind says; 'If only I could get even with the neighbour!' and 'If only I could get even with that boss!' And as they concentrate on their respective slights, rather than being on a luxurious continental divan, they might as well be on a bed of nails!

Their enemies would be amazed to know that their slights had had such far-reaching consequences. See to it that **your** opponents never steal a second of **your** valuable time!

It is strange, yet true, that whereas right-minded people would not meditate upon as unpleasant a phenomenon as excreta, they are frequently fully prepared to focus their mind upon refuse and dung of a mental calibre. It was again the Apostle Paul who said: "Whatsoever things are lovely . . . . Think on these things." (*Philippians 4:8*). However, more of that is to come in a later chapter. For the moment, I would affirm that you learn the vital lesson of being able to exclude from your mind all negative and destructive forces. You wouldn't allow an unpleasant character or a fierce dog or cat to enter your home, so why allow destructive and unpleasant thoughts to take up resident in your mind? Be alert at the door like a sentry. Never be afraid to close it speedily.

I would suggest something else. As an additional aid to switching off that which comes to harm us, let us switch our thoughts to something higher and more worthy of contemplation. You know, the conscious mind can never think of two things at the same time. So, in order to build up that impenetrable skin against unkind arrows, let me suggest that you not only reject and refuse to think further of an unkind word, thought or gesture, but that you IMMEDIATELY, think abut some truly worthwhile and, possibly, altruistic cause. Switch from the negative to the positive.

A sweet soul in a hospital ward, who seemed to have had more than a fair share of suffering, turned to me and said, "I suppose I have still many problems yet to face!" Poor soul, it appeared as if she had received the "last straw' when she heard the results of the medical diagnosis. Her weary face wrinkled, while the tears entered her eyes. My mind worked quickly, wondering what I should reply. With a smile I looked into her face. "You've faced many of life's challenges remarkably well," I said, "and knowing you, you'll accept future challenges every bit as heroically as you have those in the past." She raised her drooping head and her face lit up, "Do you think so?" she asked quizzically. I nodded.

Reader and friend, whether you interpret certain factors in life as problems or as challenges is entirely up to yourself. But just remember this: problems result in a downward stance if not a tearful eye. On the contrary, challenges raise the head and brighten the countenance. Resolve, from this moment on, that life holds no problems for you. You've replaced them with challenges!

CHAPTER III

BULLIES ONLY EXIST WHERE THERE ARE COWARDS

Although you and I will constantly be meeting folk who wish to take advantage of us, there is a factor which we must never ever forget: a word or deed unrewarded will cease to persist. Let me elaborate this. People respond to various factors in a way which time has shown to be beneficial for them. A child, for example, who does mischievous deeds and finds that such deeds draw considerable fuss and attention towards himself will soon form the habit of persisting throughout life in a highly mischievous manner. Then, if in later years he discovers that outer factors have changed and that mischievousness results in ostracism and rejection, he may well cease so to function. Should good behaviour result in appraisal and much attention, then his character may well change for the better. Of course, one must also affirm that what becomes habitual at an early age is not so easy to throw off later. When the mind is young and impressionable, before the clay of one's character has hardened, that is the time when predispositions are basically acquired and largely stay with us for the rest of our lives. Whatever sense or non-sense has been discussed in psychological circles, the influence and moulding of character which takes place during a youngster's early years must never be underestimated.

The following words of the poet Yeats should be deeply pondered, if not memorised, by every school teacher, (*Matthew 18: 5 - 7)* as well as every member of the greatest career of all time,

14

parenthood.

> *I found a piece of plastic clay*
> *And idly fashioned it one day,*
> *And as my fingers pressed it still,*
> *It moved and yielded to my will.*

> *I came again when days had passed,*
> *The piece of clay was hard at last;*
> *The form I gave it still it bore,*
> *But I could change that form no more.*

> *I took a piece of living clay*
> *And gently formed it day by day,*
> *And moulded with my power and art,*
> *A young child's soft and yielding heart.*

> *I came again when years had gone,*
> *It was a man I looked upon;*
> *He still that early impress bore,*
> *And I could change him never more.*

Let every young mother and father take these words very much to heart, for nothing can compensate for the time a wise parent spends with her offspring during an infant's most formative years than time itself. We are, indeed, thankful that human nature **can** change at any age in life, that the coward **can** become courageous, that the bully **can** be beaten, that roles **can** change and good habits can be developed, while bad habits can be discarded. **But** believe me there is one proviso: you can occasionally teach a dog new tricks when it is getting on in years, but this is hardly likely to stop it from messing the floor if it was allowed to get away with it at an age when it could have been taught better behaviour. Alas, many a bully will remain a bully for the rest of his days because of an early predisposition to act this way. However, that he should continue to act the bully and 'big boy' with yourself is a fact that can undoubtedly cease. Because a meek and gentle soul refuses to assert himself, the bully finds in him an ideal punch-bag. He gets away with hammering into such a person; and the more this wretched character can humiliate and degrade a helpless victim, the more power does this vampiric character wallow in.

The bully must dominate, and in order to do this he will seek fair means or foul. But not every such pervert will reveal his character through an open, foul expression. This kind of creature may also seek expression by, apparently, fair and respectable channels. One type will worm his way on to Church committees under the camouflage of altruistic endeavours; another type will choose occupations such as a bouncer in a night club. Basically, however, these character types are identical. The father of analytical psychology gave them the term 'anal sadistic'[1], and unfortunately they are much more common than one would wish to think. Many a lady or a gentleman with outer charm, courtesy and decorum becomes a demonic force once he or she knows him or herself to be completely the master of other folks' lives. The brutal butchers of Auschwitz, with their whips and S.S. bands, have had their counterparts in occasional psychiatric staff in the caring professions. The writer has known about them, though they do not come to light so often. It is equally his contention that some who labour in vivisection laboratories established for the supposed advancement of research could quite possibly be in those labs because they are sadists at heart.

The purpose of this chapter, however, is not so much to discuss the sadistic bully as to stop that individual from exploiting

---

1. See e.g: S.Freud. "Introductory Lectures on Psycho Analysis (Pelican edition 1973) and S.Freud "New Introductory Lectures on Psycho Analysis (Pelican edition 1973)

To this end, therefore, you must start asserting yourself. And when at first you do, you might well find all Hell let loose. Indeed, the security of one's job might be put in jeopardy - if the bully happens to be one's boss. But then, what comes first: your mental health and sanity or employment under a severely sick tyrant? Finance may indeed be a factor to consider, but health must have priority over money at every stage. The bully also can only exist vampirically. This fiend only derives satisfaction by oppressing others. And when unable to do this with you, sooner or later will turn elsewhere: the fearless cease to be victims. They are a disappointment to this sick creature's ego and the bully is forced to turn elsewhere. As I have implied, the coward alone creates the bully: the former responds to the latter's perversion, for if there were no such response from humans then there would cease to be bullies over humanity. I've no doubt, of course, that the helpless of our own as well as other species would continue to undergo torture. The writer well remembers when no more than nine years of age seeing a well-spoken and courteous neighbour giving a daily pat to his dog and then imposing upon it a merciless thrashing. The practice continued daily, and though several of the children (the writer amongst them) informed their parents, the response was similar: "It's nothing to do with us." "He mustn't be a nice person to know." "We wouldn't like to get on the wrong side of such a devious character. He could make trouble for us"! Yes, alas, bullies of the helpless animal creation exist because humans, on the whole, are too cowardly to be defenders of the defenceless. All that is necessary in this life for evil to increase is for respectable folk to sit back and do nothing!

As a clergyman, the writer is aware of several places of worship under the rule of one or two scheming power seekers. The parson, as the appointed leader, has been too gentle and kind - yes, kind to a fault - and, therefore, the Church Boards have ultimately been directed by the whims of a loudmouth whom the more refined members were not prepared to oppose. Yes, in this sense, as, indeed, in so many spheres, one can truly be nice to a fault. You need, then, to be warned of this frightful danger of being far too agreeable to others. 'Peace at all costs' defeats the object every time. For there can be no lasting peace when a tyrant, or two, disrupt a committee, or a board, in order to lord it over others.

This desire to be nice and agreeable is a weakness that the dear, gentle folk, must be at all times aware of. One needs to ask oneself: "Why am I so agreeable?" "Why do I always say 'yes' and never 'no'?" The fact may well reveal that we feel, deep down, incredibly inadequate and insecure! We crave to be liked by others. We are afraid to stand on our own two feet. May it be that we are like what was once rather naughtily said of a united gathering of Christian Prelates: 'They sit on the fence weighing up how many are on each side, and they only come down publicly upon the side where they'll get most backing!' Society is full of dumb dogs that cannot bark, just as it was in the time of Isaiah the Prophet! (*Isaiah 56:10*). There used to be a Salvation Army chorus that many a youngster learned, and many an adult would do well to learn it today:

Dare to be a Daniel, dare to stand alone:
Dare to have a purpose true
and dare to make it known!

Might I suggest that you not only stand up to the bully who confronts you but that you also give him a true minimum of your time. He is the one who will be out to pierce through your armour. See that he doesn't. And let anything he says emotionally run off your back as water from a seal. I would equally suggest that when others are with you, more time be given to them than to him. When such a tyrant begins to raise his ugly head in a meeting under the pretext of protecting the worker, the elderly, or the homeless, you'll see beneath the charade the power-seeker at work beneath it. Take it from me, such a 'character type' does not present itself at any gathering out of benevolence or philanthropy. It is basically self-centred and self-orientated to the last straw.

The ones who are the victims of such tyranny will be the kind, agreeable types, **or** the poor gullible extraverts. The latter will not as a rule see through outer charade, whereas the former types sooner or later will. Gentlemen and ladies - I mean those whose outer decorum is genuine and not a mask - have a responsibility to cultivate a more assertive and less amiable attitude towards the oppressors. They **must** learn to say 'no' and not just 'yes'; and this if for no other reason than to become assertive instead of passive. A reason for a 'no' rather than a 'yes' need never be given. You only give a reason for your decisions to your betters. You don't have to towards your equals, and certainly not to your inferiors. And in the moral and psychological scale you can be assured that most bullies are at the bottom. They are desperately sick and twisted characters.

You can, of course, always use them for your own advantage. I would suggest that though you normally keep them out of sight and mind, occasionally, for a diversion, you weigh them up objectively: notice how they seek to wield power over others and, when appropriate, play the game of giving them the impression that you haven't the ability to say 'boo to a goose' and that you're rather lacking in confidence and a trifle nervous. You'll then discover the dominance of such cruel types and the depths to which they will stoop to make you quake and buckle under. Let them have so much lead and **then**, suddenly, pull them up, showing them that you are **not** the weakling they took you for and that you can see through their little game. This usually results in them being full of apologies and assuring you that you've completely misunderstood them - which, of course, you certainly haven't! Sadly, this game played on some outwardly charming folk occasionally results in them discarding an outward mask of geniality and revealing a cruel character beneath.

19

The scriptures remind us that the heart of man is deceitful and desperately wicked; and though man foolishly judges so often by outward appearances, God looks at the heart. (*Samuel 16:7*). We shall be wise to do likewise. For many who outwardly appear as lambs are inwardly little short of ravenous wolves (*Matthew 7:15*)

To you who are desirous of 'Living life abundantly' see that these characters whose lives are 'as mustard' are treated in the same way as you would use that very condiment! Most of the time it is jarred up and kept out of sight and mind. When it faces you on the table, you can study it objectively without its effects influencing you in the slightest. It's only unpleasant when you receive too much of it inwardly - then it burns! Usually, taken in small doses and being fully recognised for what it is, it peps up that which, otherwise, could prove insipid. Well, whenever life seems a little insipid or you wish to learn a little more first-hand psychology, always feel free to analyse the bully in your presence. In doing so, you are using that character constructively, to your own advantage. The one who could have become a constant curse in your life you changed into a casual curiosity!

It has been implied that bullying, which we usually associate with a brusque, loud, forceful, and often physical expression, can just as equally be expressed in a soft emotional manner: it is equally not averse to the practice of moral and emotional blackmail. Such a bully will make a child or a spouse feel hellishly guilty for wanting to express his or herself independently. A dear soul known thirteen years ago to the writer is now a psychological misfit, and will possibly end her days in an institution because she could only start living her own form of life at the expense of an aged mother's disapproval. For the same mother's sake, the unfortunate creature had rejected an opportunity to enter a worthwhile profession. For her sake, she had declined the possibility of marriage. To avoid parental displeasure, she had also allowed her mother to choose her

20

clothes. In fact, the only escape from such frustration seemed to be in emotionally retracting. Being psychologically spineless, the poor victim's only protection was in retreating into a hard shell away from an unbearable outside world. The aged mother of that poor soul probably felt that she had been a devoted mother. Actually, she was, I dread to say it, an emotional bully who wanted others to be dependent upon her. Admittedly, I'm sure she would never have seen it that way, and the thought of telling her so would be too cruel to contemplate.

Many a spouse has inherent desires which can never be openly expressed because of the power and possessiveness of a partner. Indeed, the sexual sphere in this area may be the most obvious example. Confessed infidelity or the desire for it would be followed by such ostracism that 'outer' respectability is maintained as the norm. However, the term 'outer' is worth remembering, because the fantasizing that is linked with sexual intercourse goes far outside the marriage bed; and indeed, statistics in this sphere make it plain that the practice is frequently higher amongst women than amongst men (*See e.g. S.Dunkell "Love Lives" (Arrow Books 1980) Page 181*). Married men often hold different standards of morality at work than they do at home; and the same is frequently true when a group of women get together. Because of an overshadowing moral blackmail, dishonesty, not to mention deception, becomes the basic norm of twentieth century, British family life. Top royalty mirrors it all. Yet we dare to criticise the Victorians!

Through insight gained via depth analysis, not to mention the seal of priestly confession, the writer feels that society would be much more open and honest if partners could cast off the yoke of moral blackmail and speak honestly rather than hypocritically to each other of the sexual side of their nature. Alas, physiological vent and moral laxity are sometimes viewed as identical, and this is sometimes as misleading as equating the biological release of sex with the biblical definition of a love which seeks not its own. Eros is **not** agape!

One other factor in this category of moral blackmail comes yet to mind. The writer recalls his days spent at Oxford and sad recollections of one of those university colleges where the suicidal rate was high. And what was usually the cause in those nineteen sixties? The fear and dread in the heart of many a student of returning home to tell his Mum or Dad that he had failed them because his studying had not met with the approval of the examiners. As if any bit of paper were so valuable as to be used to determine the cessation or continuance of a life! Let no mothers or fathers reading this chapter blackmail their children, by pushing for academic attainments that could result in the forfeiture of a precious life given by God! God save us from relieving our mental inferiority by using the hard hand upon our nearest and dearest! To experience a sense of mastery and dominance which we lack elsewhere, we can so subtly become guilty of that bullying temperament we see so clearly and denounce as openly in others.

Putting into practice the relevant advice given so far will take time as well as require insight, and not a few blunders may occur. You did not cease trying, when, in learning to ride a bicycle, you grazed your knee! The end objective was well worth it. Well, so it is in the cultivation of new reaction patterns which, by enough repetition, will ultimately become as mechanical as habits. Indeed, habits are what they **will** become. Your new responses will ultimately come second nature. However, for the interim period you simply require patience and perseverance.

CHAPTER IV

ADD A PLUS AND NOT A MINUS

I haven't been out of bed all that long. The anticipation of the postman bringing some long expected mail, well overdue, has prompted me to arise quite early. Alas, the postman has just this moment passed by! 'Surely he has made a mistake!' 'Is he shirking his duties?' 'No, I can't say he is. He is quite a conscientious character.' 'I know: it's those at the other end: the office staff; or, indeed, perhaps the very one to whom I wrote.' Before long, with such thoughts simmering in my mind, I may well start this day in utter despondency with a chip upon my shoulder. And, by my manner, everyone will indirectly learn about this slight to my ego. Yes, this **could** be the way that I choose to respond to the simple fact: No post today.

If I am wise, then, I will not bring to this fact a begruntled countenance. I shall be wise to add to that the fact that I am not alone in such an experience. Very many folk have experienced such a fact. Why, I can think of not a few who might now be awaiting with anticipation a letter from myself! Yes, quite a few are overdue! How must these people be feeling? Ought I not to get down and start writing to them? Yes, I shall, and as procrastination is the thief of time, I'll start writing to them straight away; I'll use the fact that the postman passed me by as a plus and not a minus. Reader, you would be well advised to adopt the same policy; to add to the mere fact a plus instead of a minus.

It has already been mentioned that a great chunk of the writer's time is spent around hospital wards of various kinds. Most of these patients are not fully incapacitated by a long way. They could often use much of that time set aside from secular activity in writing many a long delayed letter. Time spent physically incapacitated can be put to much mental, as well as altruistic, use. Old friends, not to mention enemies, could be contacted in a truly Christian spirit. "I've conquered my enemies by making them my friends," wrote Lincoln. The time that could be used to take true stock of one's very life is an opportunity that should never be allowed to slip past. Let me again emphasise: I firmly believe that the Almighty not only allows us to fall on our backs that we may look upwards to Him; I equally believe that He wills us at times to be upset for a while in order that we may be set up for eternity!

"The man up above has saved my life for a purpose", uttered a patient; one of many whom I visited from the Piper Alpha tragedy. I knew not what to say to him; his head appeared as one brown crust; his eyes were affected - perhaps he'd never see again. And his heavily bandaged hands were fastened a little apart in a vertical position. Through much persistence I'd managed to don the respective attire: mask, apron and head gear. The medical staff had now moved to one side. They were watching on.

What was I to say apart from expressing my sympathy which anyone else could. But then the man himself, with difficulty once more spoke. "I know the Lord's Prayer; if you will say it then I'll be most pleased to say it with you". I did, and as we went through it together tears of gratitude began to flow down his cheek. Yes, that man, with others of his kind, was most thankful to have survived. He and his kind had a long way to go towards recovery. The pain they experienced from their burns was exceedingly intense. The transference of skin taken off several parts of their body would prolong the agony for several weeks ahead. The thought of buddies who had perished in the disaster would not be far from their minds. But these men of true stamina had learnt to count their blessings rather than their burdens; their gains before their losses. Otherwise, they would not have survived the pain of such burns to tell their stories.

One dear victim was undoubtedly a borderline case. "He will survive", said the Consultant, "but only if he can keep his spirits up and have the will to live. It's largely over to you, Padre!" he added, and looked intently. Well, the man did live, and the last I heard about him was that he'd become a deep reader and thinker on the purposes of his life.

One of the blessings of the old fashioned Sundays (they had their burdens too), was that one day in the week could be spent on a plane of contemplation higher than the physical and secular one. Today, one can be so very much engrossed in the affairs of the secular pursuits and activity as to be no better than a robot or a zombie.

In far off days, those living in North Wales, who were desirous of getting into England on a Sunday either had to cycle or wait until noon for the first bus. "I believe you're cycling into Chester tomorrow," stated a motorist to a teenage cyclist. "Yes, I am", came the reply. "Then there's no need to," replied the motorist; "I've to go there myself, on business and I'll gladly give you a lift both ways. It'll take two and a half hours by bike; I'll get you there in 40 minutes!" The cyclist looked at him with a smile of appreciation, but then added. "Thanks all the same but I'd rather cycle; you see, I miss so much when travelling by car!"

Well we all appreciate what the cyclist meant. Motorised transport will get us quickly from one spot to another, but at the expense of missing so much on the way. For the same reason, some would even prefer to walk. A delightful poet summed it up so well for us:

What is this life if full of care
we have no time to stand and stare.
No time to stand beneath those boughs and
stare as long as sheep and cows.

25

No time to see when woods we pass
Where squirrels hide their nuts in grass.
No time to see in broad daylight
streams full of stars like skies at night.
A poor life this if full of care
We have no time to stand and stare.
(W.H.Davies)

However one interprets religion and life, only a fool would disparage the need to set aside regular periods of time for meditation. The meaning of existence, the paths one has so far covered, and those one intends to choose, still await us. Times in which one is incapacitated physically, troubled mentally, and possibly unable to do anything else constructively, are often golden opportunities to be used for such introspection of the self.

Today the sun is shining; yesterday the clouds were very much overhead. Indeed, such is life. A sundial in an old English garden well and truly sums it up:

Sunshine and shade;
That's how our lives are made.

The sundial, in order to be of use, needs to manifest both qualities; and so indeed do we. Of course, there are those who seem to experience more than their fair share of the shade, the clouds and the storms. Believe me, they are usually the most cheerful and optimistic of people; and, having experienced tragedy of one kind or another, they are usually very keen to empathise with anyone else who is going through a stormy passage.

On the contrary, the character who has been sheltered from the clouds of life becomes no more than a sibling; and having experienced few tears in life, he becomes as spiritually and morally dry as a Sahara Desert. O yes! there may be a surface beauty about one whose life has been unruffled; but a ruffled, wrinkled face, which has weathered the storms of life courageously, has a countenance of

26

which a round characterless face is void. Consequently, those who avoid the rain, the storms and the clouds of life are hardly to be commended. They will lose so much that is spiritually vital, while those who equip themselves to ride the elements are of the stuff that martyrs, pioneers and reformers are made of. See to it, in this sphere, that you never ever choose a minus instead of a plus. Be courageous; choose courage and not cowardice.

As you learn to put the above advice into daily practice, you will find that in actual fact you are using stumbling blocks as stepping stones and life's setbacks as springboards: each daily experience and activity is for you a plus and never a minus! Your education is a never-ending process. Indeed, what you learned to equate with education at high school or university was basically no more than the assimilation of other folks' ideas; second-hand information, the conditioning and assimilation of the same being rewarded with a scroll of parchment.

The writer has many personal letters thanking him from grateful people. Is the real success of his vocation due to having studied, amongst other things, psychology, for five years? Is it because of man made ordination? For he has been in Baptist, Congregational and Anglican ministries. No, **of course not.** His usefulness is primarily because of a Divine Calling and the real education he has acquired from living. And within the latter were experiences such as losing a father at an impressionable age; losing a new-born baby; being deserted by the wife of his youth; and having a mentally retarded child. These, amongst many other factors, were the lessons experienced within the greatest school of all: 'the school of hard knocks.' I didn't say it at the time, but I can say it now: 'Thank God for the school of hard knocks!' Friend, believe me, once you have enrolled within such a school, you will actually learn to see each blot as a potential blessing, and each tragedy as a potential triumph. You know, there could be no true appreciation of light if there were

27

no darkness; there can be no appreciation of life's sunshine without its sorrow. Yes, the Master Jesus knew that without experiencing opposites many blessings could never be attained. A little fellow came across a stonemason chipping into an odd-shaped piece of granite. The worker was involved at the base of a steeple: "Why are you knocking that poor bit of stone into such odd shapes, Mister? asked the youngster, clasping his teddybear. "To fit into a niche up there, son!" came the reply. There you are: if you're a believer you'll accept it! St. Paul was, hence he could utter the words: "I am persuaded that all things work together for good to them that love God." (*Romans 8:28*) The writer believes this with all his heart, but with the proviso that the word 'ultimately' is included.

To those conversant with the message of the Old Testament scriptures, the attitude of Joseph (the man who had a coat of many colours) is an illustration worthy of consideration. Sold by his envious brothers, degraded as a slave in Egypt, raised to honour by the Pharaoh; but then wrongly accused by his wife, and, as a consequence, degraded to the lowest state. He never once complained! The years passed, and through his interpretation of dreams he was raised to the rank of Prime Minister. Years later, his evil brothers, in desperation, approached him, begging for food for themselves and their families. He was indeed unrecognised by them as the brother they once sought to destroy. But then, on his making his identity known, they are overcome by an unbearable sense of guilt and remorse. "Be not grieved that **you** sold me for it was really God who sent me, to become your deliverer" (*Genesis 45: 5 - 8*) was the gist of his wonderful reply. Joseph let no bitterness enter his system; he had used every experience as a plus rather than a minus. No wonder he could attain to Prime Minister as well as Saviour of God's chosen race!.

To those of the Christian persuasion, the example of Jesus is equally relevant. Man could do his worst with the Son of God. They

28

could bring about His crucifixion, but only because a sovereign God, moral and compassionate willed it, and used the occasion to fulfil the most benevolent act of all time *(Romans 5:8)*. Jesus, believing that a Divine goodness was ultimately in control, used every experience positively; and we would be wise to do the same. Reader, be positive with every experience and never negative.

Nineteen years ago, now, life got so strained through the writer having taken on a parish well and truly in the red, literally jinxed and fraught with disasters, that librium, and later valium, became his pills of the day. Their effects proved disastrous, side effects were unbelievable, and when his previous spouse deserted him (Who could blame her?) and he was left to keep a crumbling parish ticking over single handed, he seriously contemplated, on several occasions, taking his life. He just hadn't the courage to do it!

Fortunately for him, having also taken a critical stand against drug based conventional medicine because of its barbaric vivisection practices - as a prominent animal welfarist (once referred to on TV as the Animals' Padre!) - he had become increasingly impressed by the humane practices of alternative therapies. These included mind therapies and some had much in common with the American Congregationalist, Norman Vincent Peale, as well as the Scripture Union tapes of a Mal Garvin.

An alternative life style which provided a caring stewardship towards the rest of God's creation, the practice of positive thought, and dedication in pursuing several courses in hypnotherapy, analysis and counselling resulted in a gradual though lasting transformation. 'Why should the world have the best and most humane medications!' The Christian must always be selective, assimilating the wheat while discarding the chaff. Let that which is valuable and compatible be utilized to the greater glory of God. Medically inflicted drug dependence was discarded in no time and insurmountable difficulties were faced with a courageous optimism. He could hardly keep such a discovery to himself!

A few months passed by. The writer then found himself leading House Parties, in places as far apart as Scarborough, Whitchurch and Llandrindod Wells, to assist those undergoing the trauma of separation, bereavement and divorce. Tapes were also published for this purpose.

Top references resulted in a new post being offered and accepted; a delightfully attractive Crown living. Alas, within a fortnight the offer was withdrawn because the writer was forced into divorce against his better judgement. After having weathered two years of unwanted prominence as a deserted cleric with teenagers and an aged mother he was asked to consider an alternative offer. His boss assured him it would be by no means one of demotion but on commencement, the official title he received was that of an Assistant Curate. At first, he fumed and fretted as yet again betrayed, and this time by the Church. How childish! Those promised two years, which ended up as four, became the most appreciated years yet reached in his ministry. The folk in that Woollen Town were marvellous and the Dean, Canon Tom Sharp, the shrewdest and wisest of clerics. The writer learned a great deal from him. There was so much love and concern, and more deep friendships were forged. And then, as an extra bonus, the writer met his present wife. She, having undergone a not dissimilar experience, decided to use it constructively and became local secretary for a group of unattached Christians, each with a story to tell. Friendship, and time to study, were given in that humblest of parsonages which was a dilapidated terrace house. And here it was that study in depth, through a renowned hypnotherapist of standing, Neil French, became a daily habit. Analytical hypnotherapy was something which really worked for the writer, and, before long, others would benefit from it, too.

Dear reader, you must have had many knocks. How do you now intend to respond to them? You can use the occasions destructively as I at first did. Or you can brace yourself and respond constructively. The choice is yours. To do the former is to seal your doom. To do the latter is ultimately to be bouncing through life with vim, vigour and vitality. I know it, for that's what I'm doing each day, and you can do it too.

Your setbacks will no doubt be different from mine. Yet, whatever they are, they **can** be used constructively. Domestic problems have much in common for all of us; and so has uncongenial employment, should we be fortunate enough to have a job at all. Indeed, for those who haven't, what a grand opportunity to start up a sideline and, possibly, see it grow beyond one's dreams. What a wonderful occasion to advance one's education and to use one's talents for the benefit of others! It's **never** too late to begin, as the writer well and wonderfully knows. Dear reader, you were made to be a survivor. See to it that you not only survive, but that you soar to the heights as well. And start from today!

CHAPTER V

WEAR WHAT YOU WANT - TO BE!

Interpret the title of this chapter with limitations of course! Should you wish to become an admiral, then you would hardly be wise to don the regalia of such a person. Your reward would be far from advantageous! Nevertheless, the bride's father at a previous wedding in Aberdeen chose to attire himself in the mercantile dress of a chief engineer when in reality he had aspired no higher than that of a 'greaser' on a fishing trawler. He was probably just within the law; or maybe he wasn't! One thing **is** sure, he impressed all the guests who were present, made his daughter's day, and succeeded in clearing off to Dublin before finalising the fees for the reception. You're not advised to follow in his train! Indeed, he also bluffed the writer, who officiated, as well as the hotel proprietors, who should have made sure that fees due to them were not likely to be delayed.

It was obvious that the above man's partial success (no con man can enjoy ultimate success) was due to identifying himself with the role to which he had temporarily aspired. Such transformation, which is greatly aided by the attire one chooses as a covering, is clear for all to observe: dress in overalls or a boiler suit, and you are hardly likely to be comfortable in a boardroom of directors! Dress as a clown and you will feel a trifle out of place meditating in Westminster Abbey! Indeed, dress as a tramp and you will shortly begin to act like one; dress as a Lord and you are much more likely to move that way. It's simply the outworking of an association of idea.

One 'nutter' bluffed Bradford hospital staff in several wards because he literally identified himself with a particular consultant whom he had 'taken off' admirably. This mentally sick fellow, who had regimented hospital staff for forty minutes, was, within the very same year, stepping into the role of a newly appointed parson, before the parson himself had been formally introduced to his congregation. The writer is fully conversant with the case because he himself was the **bona fide** parson! The impersonator had 'put on' a good front; and he'd remembered to praise those whom he was conning. Folk as a rule are extremely gullible, particularly when flattery towards themselves is used.

Well now, it is not expected or anticipated that you become a con man or an actor. It is sincerely hoped that what you genuinely aspire towards you will ultimately attain - provided your aim is actually reachable, and that you're not seeking to grasp the non-existent. The purpose of this publication is to help you to bounce through life. But it is **not** to bounce you up to cloud cuckoo land! It is not only possible, but preferable, that you raise the level of your self image - with the proviso that you use it for the benefit of others as well as yourself, for none of us is an island!

Dreams can become reality, fantasy can become fact, and what you consistently identify yourself as, others must either accept you for or else part company from you. Believe in yourself, and though at first others may belittle you for your change of character and style, if you persist then you will undoubtedly win. And if success is at the cost of loosing one or two friends who wish to keep you down, then you are surely better off without them. For example, if you choose to throw off a broad uncouth accent like theirs and start speaking the Queen's English, then the effect on others may be comparable to turning on a bright light in a dusty room: dust hitherto unrecognised stands out to view! Your culture shows up their lack of it; and they will probably oppose it and may refer to you as an utter snob. They might well do both. Whether, of course, you fall for this form of pressure is entirely up to yourself. With the knowledge gained from these pages you will be forearmed for such manoeuvres, and that's half the battle won.

The choice concerning what you put on - be it clothes, accent, or stance - has the power to rejuvenate or cripple you. Take off those shabby, working clothes, groom your hair and dress yourself in your best attire. The outcome of this is that you feel quite on top! It seems as if you immediately want to stick out your chest and hold back those shoulders. Well, if that is so, then do not be afraid to spend money on well-cut and well fashioned clothing. And **please**, don't regard the latter as always being costly. Don't be taken in! The most expensive clothing is often the least appropriate and the least flattering to one's individual style: (hats and top royalty may have something to teach us here!) Look up 'top quality' clothing magazines and the attire of personalities you most admire. And learn to equate yourself with them.

We've touched upon the acquiring of a cultured accent which every soul with breeding will admire you for. But if it's an affected, 'toffy nosed' accent, you'll have only yourself to blame when folk belittle and despise you! Indeed, the very intonations of your voice reveal more than grammatical utterances. They communicate to others at a deeper level. That Victorian evangelist, D.L.Moody, was heckled because of the way he murdered the country's English language as he began to address the students at Oxford. However, towards the end of his discourse, the many jeers were replaced by many sobs. Large numbers in the crowds began to love him because he was communicating at a deeper level - to their hearts. English mattered, but sincerity meant more! If you wish to live so as to improve your own lot as well as that of others, then such sincerity will undoubtedly come across. Equally, if you wish to talk down and trample underfoot your fellow men, then this too - regardless of how you camouflage it - will undoubtedly seep through, and you will reap the contempt you deserve.

What kind of stance do you wear? Did you know that character can largely be assessed by noticing postures? O, admittedly! some dear folk, because of genetic and bodily factors, have an inappropriate stance which fails to do them justice. But posture does, time and time again, give the secret away concerning one's inner feelings and attitude. When you feel 'full of bounce' you hold your head high and your shoulders back. You walk with a gait that shows utter confidence. And as already touched upon, clothing has this helpful psychological effect. Shabbiness is hardly likely to make one prominent, unless it be used to draw attention to overcompensate for a crippling inferiority!

Well now, one needs to be assured that just as clothing greatly influences posture, and posture the mind, so even posture **by itself** can also influence the mind, and this is helpful on those occasions when prestige clothing cannot be worn! You can hardly wear the attire of an earl when your job at hand is more in keeping with a boiler suit! And that may often be so. But stance by itself can be used to affect the attitude of mind. Let me illustrate: a head held high is so associated, subconsciously, with honesty and self-esteem that the bodily 'make up' creates the mental feeling that the physical posture portrays. And once you've got that 'right feeling', you can feel, and be full of vim and vigour in almost any kind of environment!

Consider an extreme example: happiness in the mind physiologically creates a smiling face. Well, the reverse is equally correct: force yourself physiologically to smile and your mind will not stay sour for long! As the mind influences the glandular system of the body (touched upon in a previous chapter), so, equally, our physiology can have a tremendous influence over the mental state of our personalities. In your posture, and physical features, be expressive of the role you wish to pursue and the attitude you wish to attain. Identify yourself, visibly, with that towards which you are aspiring,

35

and although it seems strange when first embarked on, sufficient practice will make the 'awkwardly new' become second nature.

The writer, when a youngish man, was constantly tripping because of deformed feet, and such incidents were usually followed by swearing and inwardly fuming with rage. He later became a zealous Christian. However, whenever he tripped he had difficulty in refraining from swearing in the presence of others - a most embarrassing situation! He then decided to say "Praise the Lord!" whenever the incident occurred in the future. He would also force himself to smile as he said it. Several lapses occurred during the months that followed. Today, thirty five years later, an occasional trip brings with it a desire to utter the same affirmation. More than that, it is always accompanied by a feeling of elation.

Believe me, all that has been mentioned here is not new. Neither is it un-Christian. On the contrary, it is Biblical through and through: "Cast off the old man and be renewed in the new man", (*Ephesians 4: 22-24; Colossians 3: 9-10*) are the words uttered by St. Paul in addressing his new converts. Yes, spiritually, such a truth equally applies. And here again, faith is the operative word. 'See yourself no longer as a slave of the devil but rather as a child of the King of Kings,' is the gist of much New Testament teaching. 'Reckon your past role as now completely dead and see yourself as reborn into a new sphere.' To summarise it: visualise what you aspire spiritually to be, and live it out now with faith that God has already empowered you.

Reject 'the death instinct' that comes via pessimism and gloom. Clothe yourself with health and success. See yourself now as strong, virile, and attractive or handsome. Look at yourself in a full-length mirror and then visualise taking off all that is inferior and unworthy of yourself. Now begin in your imagination to attire yourself in superior apparel that is worthy of yourself. Cease to be an underling. No longer insult your maker by a false humility which encourages others to use you as a doormat. Begin to see your ideal self and start loving and nourishing that self. Indeed, you can never ever love your neighbour until you've learned to love yourself: and God's command to the Christian includes both. (*Leviticus 19: 18; Matthew 19:19*) Regrettably, in so many circles, there is an asceticism connected with religious piety which is a burden which weighs down the devout rather than a blessing which lifts them up. (*cp. Isaiah 46: 1 & 2 with 3 & 4*) That religion which Christ came to bring was 'good news of great joy', **not** 'bad news of big misery'. The latter, alas, is the impression that so much of Christendom conveys.

From this day onwards, wear success, love and joy. Express it through your deportment; verbalise it through your voice; convey it appropriately through your attire; and if you choose to be religious, express it through your faith!

It is to be regretted that within the past thirty years the practice of whistling has largely gone out of fashion. Indeed, during and shortly after the war years, one was confronted each day with folk who, like the dwarfs in Snow White, whistled while they worked. You knew the postman or milkman were about to call because you heard them whistling as they approached. Hollywood and Walt Disney infected Britain as well as America with the philosophy of whistling whenever an arduous task was confronted. Those animated characters from the silver screen taught us to: 'Give a little whistle'.

Thankfully, if whistling no longer appears seemly or, indeed, possible to perform, we can at least attempt to sing! Those fabulous musicals of the same screen conveyed that 'with a smile and a song', those living under the dread of invasion or death could surmount the horrors that confronted them daily. 'Ah,' you might say, 'but I can't even sing!' Then read what the Psalmist in the Good Book exhorted the chosen people of a past era to do: 'Make a joyful noise to the Lord!' (*Psalm 100*) Even the sweet singer of Israel was wise enough to know that others might not be gifted as nightingales! And talking about such a bird, remember that it is renowned for singing when it's darkest. Any bird can sing when the sun shines; you and I are called to sing at all times. Practice doing this and if you believe in the God of the Book of Job, then your acclamation will reiterate Elihu's, concerning the indifference of others: "But none says, Where is God my Maker Who gives songs in the night?"

Friend, I do not insist that you whistle today, nor do I press you to sing. I merely suggest that you be predisposed to 'make a joyful noise'. And why not accompany it with a smile? For if the former reveals contentment then the latter radiates contagion. Believe me, nothing in the world is as infectious as a smiling face. It's as expressive as the wagging tail of a four-legged little friend. In non-verbal language, it means 'I'm happy to be with you and I value your presence.'

> *'Smile a while, and while you do another smiles,*
> *and then another; and before long there are miles*
> *of smiles, and life's worthwhile; and all because*
> *of your first smile.'*

(C.England)

CHAPTER VI

TUNNELS SERVE A PURPOSE

Yorkshire is a delightful County renowned for its beautiful landscapes, its hills and valleys. However, as is to be expected, it has its fair share of long tunnels. Who could have built a railway in such an area without having tunnelled through hills to come out into further valleys? One such tunnel holds a soft spot for the writer, it reminds him of times when he travelled from Lancashire to Yorkshire, and though it was quite an experience on the train to be plunged into a long period of darkness the light and beauty which one witnessed on resurfacing was a glorious sight to behold. That particular tunnel was a great feat in workmanship because the navvies who had built such a lengthy expanse through the Pennines were only equipped with the tools and implements of a bygone era. Indeed, many of them would never live to see the completion of their work. Most were of Irish stock, desperate to find employment of any kind. Yet such rough and ungainly navvies were not without a Faith which meant so much to them. The years taken tunnelling through that rock seemed never ending, and as for coming out into the light at the end of each working day, the leisure hours were few and the distance was often too far to traverse to witness the light. However, they were hardy men for though they were enveloped by darkness they made the most of their situation. A cavern was created far within one of those tunnels; there was a canal as well as two tracks to consider; and this vast vault became not only a place to rest and sleep;

39

it also became a rallying spot for worship; for their offering of the Mass. Yes, they transformed a cavern of darkness into a cathedral for worship and from it they received spiritual illumination and sustenance with which to labour on. One couldn't help but feel a lump in one's throat as one considered those far off workmen; and all so that busy trains could rattle as Transpennines, escorting people from one famous county to another.

Reader, if you are compelled to work for any period of time within a dark and uncongenial atmosphere just think of those poor creatures with a lamp or candle in the nib of their cap, and rock dust in their lungs, the trickle of water round their feet and a dampness and clamminess round their body which had their clothes sticking to them.

No doubt, their thoughts were mostly of far off days way back in Ireland of relations, friends, and children whom they would possibly never see again. Yet, they used a vast cavern as a temple to God and they would realise with a simple childlike faith that they were not alone. A great spiritual light must have emanated on Sundays and holy days from that cavern within the deep bowels of darkness. Dare you or I moan at our petty setbacks when we compare our lot in life with theirs? How dare we!

Human beings love to moan and often do until they consider life from the perspective of others:

'I had the blues because I had no shoes,' cried one. Until
'Down the street, I met a man who had no feet!'

If you have been a victim of self pity and considered that life had too many tunnel experiences to undergo then put yourself at the side of others. 'But I've never had a fair chance!' says one. Then what about a whole host of others: for example, the great Helen Keller, deprived of both hearing and sight and yet through the dedication of another, whose name is generally unknown, established homes and institutions worldwide for the blind. If ever one was in perpetual darkness it was she; yet from that darkness a tremendous light has ever shone since her day. Braille has been taught to millions and new hope given to both blind and deaf.

Think of yet another creature who was forced to undergo a never ending tunnel experience through life, Fanny Crosbie. From six weeks old she had been deprived of her sight, and all through a charlatan of a healer calling on her mother and telling her to put poultices on her baby's eyes to cure a passing affliction. The child who had seen the light of day was now to be denied it for the rest of her days. Did she frown, fume and rage? No! When merely five or six she wrote a little poem:

'O what a happy girl am I although I cannot see,
I am convinced while in this world so happy I shall be!'

There you have it! Didn't I speak previously about interpretations being of far more importance than facts? Fanny grew up to be one of the greatest hymn writers of all times. She wrote around two thousand. Who hasn't heard of 'Blessed Assurance', 'To God be The Glory', 'I am Thine O Lord', and 'Rescue The Perishing'? One day, Fanny was able to witness to her Faith while visiting a prison. One of the inmates felt that life had been unduly harsh and unfair with him. But after he'd listened to the old lady who had to be escorted in and out before she could speak, seeing the radiance and gratitude for life that emanated from this lovely soul, the prisoner was overheard to say within earshot of Fanny, 'Dear Jesus, please don't pass me by'. For she'd been preaching on blind Bartimeaus! The dear saint of God made her way home and compiled yet another hymn to her list, 'Pass me not O gentle Saviour'.

It may be, of course, that the tunnel you're going through is not literal darkness; indeed, if it were you'd hardly be reading this book. But whatever it is, shun self-pity as you would the plague itself; and, of course, if you want a Divine example, there's Jesus Himself: brought up by a poor peasant couple, gossiped about as illegitimate by the very religious elite, (*John 8:41*) unable to secure the basic education due to His responsibility in being the bread winner for a widowed mother and younger brothers and sisters, (*Matthew 1:25 & 13: 55-56*) forsaken at the last by his friends except for the youngest, denied by one, betrayed by another, he has, nevertheless altered the whole course of history, for even those who refuse Him allegiance are forced to acknowledge him whenever they write down the date!

Tunnels, yes, they were forged by many who sacrificed their lives through their making! Yet for us who use them they now serve a wonderful purpose. Imagine the journey across the Pennines without a railroad! O yes, it's possible and the writer has taken it many times; but for speed, smoothness and safety the tunnel must take priority every time. That's why it was built and long before zigzag climbing and descending **modern** roads were ever thought of. Yes, the purpose of the tunnel is to transform an arduous and sometimes unsurmountable journey into a short one! Its analogy to the moral and spiritual world remains true for all time.

Dark patches teach us to trust when we cannot see: they teach us to look beyond ourselves to a greater presence whom we'd never search for while it's light. The writer's youngest child is mentally backward but this is not to imply he is not bright. One day the train rattled into the darkness of the Stanedge Tunnel and young James, for that is his name, felt as a mere twelve year old then a trifle nervous. He began to get more and more disturbed, and especially as the haze from the tunnel entered a window that was not fully closed. "Daddy, are you alright?" he asked, and seemingly my reply was not clear enough for him. The question was repeated the second time but with further emphasis, "Daddy are you sure you are alright?" His smiling, jovial yet questioning face looked more attentively at me. "Yes, James," I said, "I'm alright," and I clasped his hand. His face shone like the sun; he put his finger in his mouth and sat back relaxed. Dear reader, forgive me but there's a moral in that story for you. In the darkness of life's tunnels, when gloom and haze surrounds and we know not what is happening, you and I have a Father at our side. All we need to do is call to Him and if He hasn't replied the first time then we would be wise to call a little louder the next. He has in fact replied; it's just that with the clamber and sound of the world without that we don't always hear Him within.

Although nothing seems to compensate, at least not in the mind of a railway enthusiast, for the smell of smoke and the sound of steam, the tunnel experience is often the exception. Inability to see in front, plus the soot and the grit which blackens the face and troubles the eye results in many preferring a tunnel trip in a diesel train rather than in an old time steamer. Like the metros or the tubes it's an exciting experience, awaiting the first glimmer of that pin prick of light in the distance and watching it getting larger and larger until one is almost bolted out into a brilliance which for a moment or two truly dazzles the eyes. Yes, it turns dull darkness into excitement, focusing the eyes on that ever growing yet far away pinhead of light! So, similarly, whatever darkness or despondency one is temporarily submerged in, it is helpful to look round searchingly for a tiny glimmer of light. Look long enough and you **will** see it while all around is darkness; but as you focus your gaze upon it other things will become obscure and, unnoticeable. Whatever the mind focuses its gaze upon, then that is the thing that will become clearer and larger. From a pinprick perception it will grow until it encompasses you and you are a part of it. Alas, far too many in this life are obsessed by floaters in their eyes than in the gorgeous landscape ahead of them; they're more attentive to the tinnitus of their ear than to the symphony outside of it. Such afflictions are common to most of us - if not when young then certainly with the passing of the years! - but the moral is that the more we focus or tune in to them the more out of proportion do they become. Yes, like a pampered and spoiled child, the more of our attention they then demand!

A skilled hypnotist, with a willing subject, can get the participant to so focus the attention as to narrow down and intensify the field of view or sound as to have the subject completely oblivious to everything else except that which he requests the client to experience. Indeed, the very word 'hypnosis' was faultily coined by a physician called Braid. He later realized that the phenomena was not a state of sleep and drowsiness; but actually a state of narrowed concentration and heightened awareness which temporarily enveloped the whole of the individual attention. In all fairness to him he then sought to alter the name of the condition to 'monoedism' but, by that time, the faulty name had caught on and regrettably had come to stay for all time. The implication of this remark is that though surrounded by a whole host of stimuli encroaching upon us, only what we focus on or tune into becomes the relevant and 'seeming' real.

Unpleasant factors, physical as well as mental may well push to make their presence felt, but unless the cause is a gripping appendix or a violent toothache, we would do well once we have registered its warning and acted upon it, to then give it the least attention possible. If your tooth jibs then ring the dentist to confirm an appointment, you'll then do well to divert your attention elsewhere. I'm sure that if a sudden surprise of a win on the pools followed, or even the news of a tragic and sudden loss, then the unpatted tooth in your mouth would settle down until a more opportune time came to represent itself.

Yes, the dark tunnel on being left behind seems to temporarily make everything uncannily bright and colourful. Every experience in life has its compensations though we don't always realise it. What a meaningless drab world it would be if we never witnessed the dark and lived perpetually in the light! The Good Book says: 'The Almighty made darkness as well as light, night as well as day and it

also says that everything he made was good' (*Genesis 1:18 & 31*)
You probably appreciate the light but hardly the darkness; yet if there
was no night then life on this planet would cease to exist; that's a
scientific fact and not a scriptural one. But morally and spiritually too
the truth remains, as already touched upon, that a life lived with
constant sunshine ahead would become as barren, and fruitless as the
Sahara. Variety is the spice of life and this must include a balanced
mixture of light and darkness.

Yorkshire is a vast county of variation and contrasts. It has its
areas of idyllic and superb beauty! Yes, and in the words of the late
John Betjeman it has in other parts that strange 'beauty of ugliness!'
Yes, indeed, there is such a paradoxical beauty. Not far from those
gorgeous hills and valleys, which are sometimes joined by dark
tunnels, there stand the dark remains of partly used or else partly
derelict mill workings. The silent or sleepy mill near the canal, with
a cool and stagnant pond at its side, is as a ghost from the past. It is
an uncanny silence, undisturbed except for the sound of a thrush or
a linnet, conveying a sanctity unique to itself and a reminder of
harder, often cruel and yet often more satisfying years, when men and
women, rightly or wrongly, were more satisfied with their lot in life
even though the money was poor and the hours of labour were so
long. Did I not say in the second chapter that attitudes are greater
than facts? But then, not every mill at the side of the deserted canal
is derelict or dead. One such mill, the writer remembers was vibrant
with activity. As one was to pass a certain shed there was, indeed a
deafening sound. Through the open door one witnessed those
special people, the weavers busy at their work. Why, their inability
to hear each other had resulted in them evolving a method of lip
reading. You'd to guard your mouth when a weaver was around!
There they worked with a whole lot of entangled and coloured
threads, some bright and others dark, yet all vitally necessary for the
work they were furthering while those noisy shuttles were cata-

45

pulted at a frightful speed from side to side. It all reminded me of life's experiences, and the shuttles going to and fro, of our years that so speedily come and go.

My life is but a weaving between my Lord and me.
I cannot choose the colours He worketh steadily.
Oft times He weaveth sorrow and I in foolish pride
Forget He sees the upper while I the under side.

Not till the loom is silent and the shuttles cease to fly
Shall God unroll the canvas and explain the reason why.
The dark threads are as needful in the Weaver's skilful hand
As the threads of gold and silver in the pattern He has planned.

(Anon)

Dear reader. Those mills have a message for us as well as those dark tunnels; remember the moral whenever you pass either; let them be as visual aids on your great journey through life.

CHAPTER VII

YOU BECOME THE EXPRESSION
OF YOUR DREAMS

The Divine Book reminds us that as a person 'thinketh in his heart, so is he!' (*Proverbs 23:7*) I'm sure we know this without recourse to such a volume. If one wishes to know another's character, just take note of what most engrosses his mind. Watch his bookshelf, her magazine rack and their choice of programmes. You have the answer; it is as simple as that! It is hardly surprising that Ian Brady and Myra Hindley, those notorious Moors Murderers, had indulged their minds for some years previous to the atrocities for which they were convicted, studying from cover to cover publications such as those of the Marquis De Sade. And indeed, moving from one extreme to another, it is equally not surprising that Francis of Assisi dwelt on the sufferings of Jesus for so long that eventually the stigmata appeared on his body.

In order that the body might materialise the mind's aims and aspirations, a blueprint first of all needs to be established and this will then become the goal that the psyche strives to create and the body adapts to. Build up constructive thought pictures; see yourself as you wish to become; and as you temporarily do menial tasks, always keep that ideal picture constant within your mind. Indeed, what you truly visualise and anticipate you are three quarters of the way to actualising. The Good Book of the Christian calls it faith, and its Founder said, "Whatever you require, believe that you have it, and you will receive it." (*Mark 11:24*) In other words, you behave just as though it had already materialised; and, indeed, to you it will! The moment, of course, that you doubt, then you are working against it. Indeed, such far off Biblical teaching is identical to the requirement laid down for successful auto suggestion; and in this respect the writer believes that to call Jesus a utilizer of what we term today hypnotherapy would be more akin to truth than to blasphemy.

It needs to be mentioned that the emphasis, in such a context, must always be placed upon the imagination, and never upon the will. It is the former that creates emotion; and when our emotions, through what we have dreamed, pull one way and the so-called will power pulls the other, then the emotions will win every time. This is, indeed, an indisputable psychological fact and was first clarified by the father of what was then the new Nancy school of hypnosis, Emile Cou'e. He said, "In the conflict between the Will and the Imagination, the force of the Imagination is in direct ratio to the square of the Will [1]" To illustrate: You may have the willpower to climb dizzy heights up a precarious ladder, yet, as you do so, your feet shake at the thought of what a fall entails. You get half way and, on looking down, you see the midget traffic beneath and, on looking up, you see the whirling sky above. And the consequence is, that with the best will in the world, you become frozen to the spot, unable to do one thing or the other.

Trying is of the will and is as fruitless as trying to sleep. It defeats the object. Whereas visualising an appropriate slumberland scene promotes it.

With regard to Emile Cou'e, most folk have remembered him for those famous and oft-repeated words to be constantly re-

---

1. See e.g. C.H.Brooks. "Practice of Auto Suggestion by the method of Emile Cou'e (George Allen & Unwin Ltd. (1922) Page 65.

affirmed, and preferably visualised, void of every effort of the will: 'Every day and in every way I get better and better and better.' Indeed, if those who are constantly swallowing tablets, assimilated into their minds positive phrases as often as they do drugs into their stomachs, then most of the beds in our hospitals would be empty. Instead of brooding and imagining the worst until it materialises, we ought, by our optimism, to be bringing about the materialisation of a superb and zestful personality. The choice, dear reader, is yours; in a very real sense, you are still the master of your destiny.

Two types of people constantly seek the help of the writer: the type whose life is focused upon defeat; and the type whose life is focused on victory. The former spend most of their time counting their burdens; while the latter are predisposed to count their blessings. The pessimist and the optimist exist in community life side by side.

The latter is welcome wherever he goes, for his joy is infectious. Indeed, the former is also infectious and that's why he usually ends up on his own: who wants the company of a sourpuss? Of course, there are those whose profession includes caring for these poor morbid introverts. The well remunerated social worker is involved in their practical needs. But the poorly paid parson is usually expected to share their past recollections, with the district nurse! A wise cleric seldom asks such folk how they are feeling. He knows the answer! Though he has many others to visit of a more congenial disposition, a request for a sick visit, or for Holy Communion from a dear, frail soul who can no longer get to the church (yet, remarkably, makes it to the Darby and Joan!) can hardly be ignored.

The parson, the doctor, the neighbour, or whoever else visits this particular type of creature, is likely to be offered a cup of tea with eatables. Who dares now to say that she has no thought for others, but only for self? Alas, one cannot make a speedy exit when refreshments are so kindly provided. It seems common courtesy to become a human sponge, absorbing one morbid horror story after another. **Or does it?** Believe me I am not hard when I say that the least time you spend in such company the better for your own sanity, as well as theirs. Spend a minimum of your time with a pessimist and a moaner; and use every moment of it to encourage, with genuine enthusiasm, any positive, cheerful, utterance they might give.

There is a mentality which also loves to swap horror stories: whatever your aches, pains and problems, they have worse to return. Woe betide you if you deflate their ego by having had a worse story to narrate to them than they have been able to pass on to you!

Cease playing horror tapes of **your** past life too! Get away from the fog and the gloom, and focus your attention on the sunny side of life. Visit the downcast only to lift them up, but see to it that they don't gain the mastery by pulling you down! Face all experiences, from this moment onwards, as though you were on top of them. Facts are facts and, understandably, you may, paradoxically, have some subordinate if not inferior roles to perform on life's journey. Well, never be ashamed of that! Though prelates may be living in palaces, remember Jesus Christ was a manual worker who lived in a peasant's workshop. Let Him be your example for, poor as He was by the world's standards, He was truly 'The Master' in each and every situation. 'And why was this?' you ask. Well, amongst other things, He never set too high a standard on His dearest friends; He was ready for the worst to which they might stoop. He hadn't confined His Love to one or two; for He knew that when some would forsake Him, others wouldn't. His love, the greatest as far as Christians are concerned, was never gullible. Madison Avenue publicity tricks, such as a kind face or a courteous voice, would not have deceived Him (*Matthew 7:15*). Jesus held reservations, for He knew human fickleness as well as guile. He held reserves too! When earthly companions failed Him, He had friends in the Glory above with whom to converse. (*e.g. John 16:32*)

50

Then see to it, in matters of human love, that you never put all your eggs of affection and love into but one basket. Let your love be noble sincere and true, but never be possessed by anyone. And never become gullible to the subtleties, frailties, and so often the fickleness, of that misused four-letter word: love. Should your head be in the clouds, see that your feet are always firmly on the ground.

In order to fulfil those dreams and to be in control of each situation, present yourself with utter confidence; for you are a child of the Universe if not the King of Kings. Others will try the power game upon you, and this might be expressed in a number of ways. When they shake your hand, they might well turn their hand on top of yours: they really want to dominate you! When they invite you into their office, they might well have the light intentionally glaring down on you as they take a subdued position. They may be keen to give advice but reluctant to receive it. In other words, they are pictorially talking down to you. They might even have the audacity to sit in comfort while you stand or sit perched on a hard chair. And they are hoping that you will fall into the role of submission within the picture they've mentally sketched. Watch out for such manoeuvres and treat them as infantile, which indeed they are.

Seventeen years ago, and within the same month, the writer underwent two interviews in London. The first concerned enquiries into government work as a chaplain. A room was entered, and on a raised platform sat a group of interviewers who asked him to sit on a hard chair while they from above fired a series of gruelling questions. Then, when the interview was over, a suggestion was made that if the interviewee would walk along the corridor outside, he would discover a tea machine, but that he would need some coins to operate it. A couple of weeks later the other interview occurred, this time in no less a place than 10 Downing Street. The Prime Minister's secretary for ecclesiastical Crown appointments was the interviewer (*Mr. C.V.Paterson, Secretary for Appointments, Sept.*

1979). His kindness and courtesy were more than ample. A choice of refreshments having arrived, the maid was courteously dismissed and the interviewer himself took the role of a first-class host, pouring out the tea and passing eatables. Yes, two unique types of power had been met within the same month.

You are acquiring power to bounce through life. How do you intend to use it? To break or build another; to belittle or boost? Strangers pass through our lives most days; and most of them will never return. What kind of power do we exert before them? It may well be that our task is to judge the character of others. Let it never be forgotten that in the process we also are judged and our characters laid bare. When pointing one finger at another three are pointed back!

Are others encouraged by our power? Are they that bit better because they've encountered us? Abraham Lincoln, while a young man, dreamt dreams and as an adult he received power to enact them. The following words have been attributed to him:

> *'I expect to pass this way but once*
> *any good thing, therefore that I can do*
> *or any kindness that I can show to any creature*
> *let me do it now. Let me not defer or neglect it*
> *for I shall not pass this way again.'*

Dear reader, you are now well into this book and I suggest your daily dreams include two most vital factors: health and success. They will be of benefit to you directly and to others indirectly. Begin then to visualise their actualization. Speak about them positively and learn to anticipate them each day. When ready for sleep, why not count the occasions when such benefits have come your way? If you're a believer, do not hesitate to count them as you are able, thanking your Maker for them. Wonder of wonders, you'll find that no week passes by without several more to add to the total - that's if ever you could total them all! Remember the chorus that goes:

'Count your blessings, name them one by one,
Count your blessings, see what God has done?'

Then might I suggest you, 'Count your blessings, name them by the score, and it will surprise you there are thousands more!'

CHAPTER VIII

DON'T BE SWAYED BY THE SPINELESS!

Very many folk possess a will comparable to a weak backbone. And some, indeed, possess no backbone at all! The former need support and the latter retreat into a shell. Let me illustrate the former first of all and then we shall discuss the latter.

People who feel a trifle insecure will constantly ask others for their opinions, not so much to compare these opinions with their own, a commendable practice, but rather to find out if their own opinion is acceptable to another. They are afraid of being 'way out' and subject to social rejection or possible ridicule. While entertaining some views of their own, they lack the initiative to act upon them lest they be considered by the majority as odd and eccentric. They are only prepared to follow their own conscience and light if it is accepted by the group with whom they associate. They lack conviction in what they propose; and what is more common, they are afraid of stepping out of line lest, in doing so, they are rejected by the herd of humanity. Such folk must have the support, the crutch or splint of others. They are never strong enough in character to weather the storms and gales which arise when one goes contrary to general and accepted opinion.

If you are of the temperament touched upon in the above paragraph then you'll not become a Lincoln, a Wilberforce, a Gladys

Aylward or a Mother Theresa! You would never end up as a pioneer, and certainly not a martyr, if your life's work and aspirations are conditioned by seeking approval from others. However, the majority are still like sheep without a shepherd; and if **you** choose to be different and have sufficient backbone, then you may well be the kind of shepherd others are looking for. The masses are not aware of it, but lacking confidence and initiative themselves, they look for a leader to lean on, follow and sometimes blame!

You, the reader, were certainly not created to be just a cog in the mechanism of a heartless society; you might well be, potentially, a pioneer. One thing is imperative; being desirous of bounding through life without bruising easily, you must firmly grasp the helm of your own barque. Believe me, if you don't, then others will steal the helm from under your very nose and steer your life to suit their own ends, and nothing is more certain than that. Those Abraham Lincolns and Gladys Aylwards of the past were firstly masters of their own destinies and, as a corollary, they became masters of philanthropy. It is comparatively easy for us to pursue paths of liberation and emancipation which they forged against 'respectable' opinion. The path of the follower is comparatively easy. As for the pioneers, they were often 'up against it' not only from mercenary-minded and aggressive mobs, but also from the epitome of moral respectability. Indeed, William Wilberforce found some of **his** strongest protagonists within the very House of Bishops. But was it not similar with Jesus Christ?

When the outwardly evil oppose your objectives, you may have cause to be glad. But when the moral mouthpieces of society castigate you as a rebel and 'a stirrer of the people' then unless you have the character that the saints and reformers were made of, you will easily succumb for social approval. It's so easy to prefer the friendship of the group rather than the peace and blessing of a good conscience. if not, indeed, the Smile of one's God.

Never be deceived into thinking that even the majority are right. The blunders of democracy are there for all to see. The Christian religion, which has conquered the Western world, was pioneered by a dozen semi-literate peasants from the backwoods of Palestine. Buddhism, which came much earlier, was of a not unsimilar origin. It was Winston Churchill who said to a Nazi leader: 'Never underestimate the influence of minorities'. On the contrary, the majorities who have claimed to be right because of numerical power, have often manifested themselves in bloody revolutions and the chaos and bawdiness of city councils!

Concerning those who are spineless, and as a consequence retreat into their shell, they are constantly being bumped into! The shell into which they retreat is sometimes one of fantasization: having no backbone for this outer hard and cruel world they often become avid bookworms or T.V. addicts. If their choice of book is the novel, then they'll often find themselves identifying their own personality with the noble hero of fiction. The fact is that it's much easier to be a hero in a make-believe set-up than in the real world of hard knocks and living reality.

Other such character types may have more sympathy with the history of social reform. They will know all about the heroes and heroines of a past era. Alas, the awful tragedy is that rather than use such knowledge to spur them on to do similar work in their own generation, they get no further than reading about it. Discussion, if not fantasy, becomes so very sadly a substitute, rather than a spur, for individual action.

These well-intentioned folk will spend many hours discussing the case 'for' or 'against' needed reforms. However, that individual action should follow on a practical level appears to them as quite irrelevant. Obviously, they find the outer world too hard to face, so all sorts of rationalisations follow as a subconscious means of avoiding the actual activity of doing something about it. Should the cause, for example, be that of animal cruelty, then the excuse will be that humans must come first; and if it be the Third World you'll be told in no uncertain terms that charity must begin at home. If vegetarianism be the menu (and who wouldn't be with B.S.E!) concern will be expressed for the livelihood of the meat producer! Their excuses are often **ad infinitum**. But they all have the desired subconscious effect: no action is ever taken one way or another.

The task of the reader of this work is to be aware of those subtle schemes and strategies of others and to observe and recognise them for what they are - even though the ones who manifest them may be fully unaware of the psychological processes and rationalisations taking place. Your task, then, is never to condemn them, but just to notice and observe, 'for they know not what they do'. Be always aware that what is being rationally discussed on the intellectual surface is being influenced by factors beneath the surface level of the mind.

Well now, are you going to be swayed by some of those nice, gentle and yet, so often, spineless folk? Indeed, that they are so nice and gentle is often the hardest part to bear! If they were not apparently sympathetic to your own personal interests, then you would soon tell them to 'get off'. But how can you, when they seem, so often, to have your own welfare at heart? A wise man once uttered this prayer:

> *'Lord, I can look after my enemies.*
> *I ask you to save me from my friends*
> *Amen'*

What wisdom there is in such a petition! "Don't get involved in that cause . . . You may well get into trouble . . . They're only using you to do what they haven't the guts to do themselves". "They're making the bullets for you to fire!" "You need to look after your health . . . You could get pneumonia if you venture out in this". "It's high time you took life easier; you owe it to yourself". Such is the pattern of advice that friends so often give us. If we're wise, we'll sort out the wheat from the chaff.

Though we'll be wise to appreciate and value the warmth of friendship that is anxious to keep us from being hurt, we will nevertheless remain fully at the controls, and we'll see to it as much in life as in motoring that we are never, ever, flummoxed by back-seat drivers!

Jesus once uttered these strange and perplexing words: 'Except a man hate his mother, father, wife and children, and his own life also, then he cannot be my disciple'. (*Luke 14:26*) I must admit that I found the words hard to reconcile with the example of Christ's own life. However, with the hindsight of the years, I now see the meaning as clearly as the light of day. Top priority must be given to that still, small, inner voice of conscience. And if this is adhered to, then, on rare occasions, one must go contrary to the persuasions of those closest, unsupported except with one's conscience as a guide. That most famous of literary allegories, *Pilgrim's Progress* tells in its opening pages of Christian leaving the lower city in search of the higher one, and as he leaves the City of Destruction, his wife and children, as well as goodly neighbours, come out to plead with him to turn back from pursuing his course. He is compelled, as it were, to put his fingers into his ears; he looks towards the goal and cries out for all his worth, 'Life, Life, eternal Life!' Well, our aim may not be a Celestial City above, though it could very well be! But, in an effort to live life nobly and fully we need the utmost courage of our convictions, and a determination never to be sidetracked from the goal.

Some folk do have some fairly strong convictions. They will stick out their necks so far, but never enough to achieve anything worthwhile. Though they make a commotion over certain facts, in reality, they are little better than yapping puppy dogs on a lead. They make a protest, but it soon ceases when a tug is felt on the lead. The holder of the lead could be 'respected society'; 'the moral norm of one's group'; 'the feelings of one's family'; or the response of one who considers his or her viewpoint wiser, and has the arrogance to assume it.

Jesus knew all about such tugs. His friend Peter discredited the thought that He would ever entertain death by crucifixion (*Matthew 16:22*). His mother, brothers and sisters thought He was going out of His mind, and on one occasion sought to restrain Him (*Mark 3:21 & 31*). But though these protests may have tugged on His heart strings, He was nevertheless not to be side-tracked from His goal. Neither friends nor foes could frustrate the plans He was inwardly called to fulfil.

Dear friend, dare to believe, if necessary, that everyone else could be wrong and that you alone are right. Remember not only the example of Jesus, but think of the pilgrimage of Columbus, who dared to believe that the world was round instead of flat. Have the equal confidence of a Galileo who, in total opposition to an authoritative Church, claimed that the sun rather than the world was the centre of our universe.

You were surely born **not** to be moulded by society but to mould it for your own good and the betterment of all life upon it. You were meant to take full control of your life. Then start doing so from today.

CHAPTER IX

THE NARROW OPENING INTO THE BROAD HIGHWAY

As a youngster, the writer used to pass through a narrow side-gate in order that he might come out into a broad thoroughfare. And is not that a fitting analogy of entrance into living life to the full? It is usually via a narrow approach. Indeed, the Founder of Christendom knew all about it when he said, 'Narrow is the path that leads to life and few there are who find it'. *(Matthew 7:14)* Yes, the majority of folk could hardly be viewed upon as walking the highway of life's fullness. A mere existence would be more appropriate as a term for their life than that of eternal life, or Life with a capital L!

One is Biblically expected to enter eternal life here and now. To think of it as something reserved for the Hereafter is to misinterpret the teaching of Jesus of Nazareth. He came that people of His day might cast aside the shackles of serfdom, as well as those of religious bondage, by practising the great truths of living positively with a Faith that overcomes worldly obstacles. It was, and is His Wish that this fullness of life be experienced by you. And the cost involved is that - in certain spheres - you deny yourself temporarily in order that you may be more than compensated in the future. You haven't to await an existence beyond the grave for this to transpire! That master Guru of Christendom was a realist concerned with life here and now, and only to a much lesser extent did He touch upon the subject of the Hereafter.

Bearing, then, such factors in mind, it is vital that we accept the temporary inconvenience of a narrow path passing through a narrow gate, because it comes out into a life of broadness and of freedom. You see, whether one likes it or not, physical, mental and moral, as well as spiritual fullness can only come via antecedent restrictions.

In order that you may appreciate this great Truth, it will be helpful to consider the simple analogies that follow.

To enter an ice rink and, as a spectator, view the grace and charm of some of those professional and semi-professional skaters is truly a spectacle worth viewing. Why the very ice under their feet seems subject to their control! They appear to be masters of the rink and they use it with a grace and freedom which leave us almost breathless.

Perhaps you and I are anxious to follow suit. So what do we do? Why, we enter the ring and immediately fall with a hard bump upon the ice! We get up with difficulty, rub our posteriors, and make our way homewards (at least, here I'm rather speaking of what I once did myself!). But as for those skaters who express themselves with such ease, it was obvious that though they must have experienced bump after bump, they bounced back, refusing to give in. They were not deterred. The fact that today they find skating such joyous freedom, while the writer finds it so hellishly difficult, is merely that for very many hours in the past they denied themselves such freedom when the writer didn't! The former were passing through temporary restrictions in order that they might later enjoy the freedom of an ice rink. The latter, though once fond of the rink, rejected temporary restriction for a past broadness to do whatever he then wished. Alas, for him, now, there can be no freedom on the ice rink, only restriction and fear of 'leaving go' of the rail at the side.

Have you got the message? Then we'll pass on from the freedom of one bodily pleasure to another, which, though expressed through the body, is primarily the effect of a disciplined mind.

The writer's close friend is one who lives - to an extent no one else known to him has done - full of vim, vigour and vitality. David Windle makes an organ play as no one since Reginald Dixon has ever done! He plays in places such as Blackpool's Tower Ballroom; for people such as Ken Dodd, and has been on tours world wide. The wonder of this musician is that he has such versatility as to be every bit as much at home on Dewsbury Minster's organ for Harry Secombe as on a Welsh chapel organ accompanying the writer. And he plays equally as well without a script as with one.

What has been the cause of such brilliance? What is the secret behind such success? It certainly wasn't a hereditary factor. Neither was it influenced by social or educational privileges. The basic and prime factor is this: when other teenagers were enjoying freedom in the streets, this fellow would lock himself into a Huddersfield Parish Church of the back streets; and, indeed, he practised boring scales often for hours at a time. You see, he imposed upon himself teenage restrictions. Shall we say that he chose to travel through the restrictions and confines of a narrow path with a restrictive gate? And his reward, later, is a musical freedom that anyone hearing would truly covet!

But now, let's pass on to the same process with moral and spiritual factors before us. The alcoholic has chosen the broad gate; he has thrown out restrictions. So, indeed, has the drug addict; and so, similarly, has the sexually promiscuous. But the question I put to you is this: has such a broad gate brought freedom? Are such folk living on the broad highway of liberty? Can one with any stretch of imagination say that such examples of humanity are bouncing through life with vim, vigour and vitality? You know the answer without the writer giving it to you. They have no more lasting joy and freedom than a slave. Their master is their own particular obsession. Rather than use drink, sex or drugs to serve them, they are its bond slave.

Life's intended servants have become tyrants and taskmasters. The virtue of moderation is unknown to an addict, for rather than be at the helm of his appetites he is constantly at their mercy. The sun may shine in its beauty; the birds may sing above; the children may be playing in the meadow; but the addict is blind and deaf to them all. He only exists to try and quench his appetite that can never, ever be satisfied. Because he refused past restriction in preference for a broad gate at the beginning, he is now rigorously restricted for the rest of his earthly sojourn.

As a narrow and restrictive beginning blossoms out into a broad highway, so must the reader practice the advice given in these pages. Knowledge is little use unless you begin to put it into practice. You **must** put such advice into operation, and - I'm sorry to say it, but it has to be said - some of this practice will create temporary inconvenience. You are going to be misunderstood; you may even be opposed; your ex-superiors and masters are not going to like your new behaviour though, thankfully, a few exceptions will admire you from the start. However, regardless of whether others begin to scowl or smile towards you, one thing is sure; you are going to begin admiring yourself as never before! Success **will** lead to success, **but**, temporary unpleasantness, discipline and restraint are the prices you **must** accept and expect.

Friend, you have decided to digest and practice the advice given here, well, for the next few months the cost to yourself is going to be comparable to passing along a narrow path with a very restrictive gate! However, paradoxically, the compensations will be felt too; you'll soon be on a broad highway.

The college student is spurred on to discipline and self-mastery because a diploma or degree, as a red carrot, is dangled before him: a career - where life can be lived on a new and exciting level - awaits him. Why, it's well worth a temporary time of discipline; of doing things that go a little against the grain. Reader, your reward is not one qualification; it will be many: to stand on one's own feet; to put cowards in their place; to unashamedly express one's opinions; to see through the subtle strategy of others; to protect the defenceless; to give troublemakers the exit they deserve, and to organise one's time. Indeed such factors, to quote but a few, are well worth the inconvenience and awkwardness felt from introducing new thought forms and behaviour patterns into one's life.

You will realise that the time taken, and the hours used, in digesting this small volume will bring dividends that will later amaze you. You will be able to look back in retrospect and be ever grateful that this publication once came into your possession. Should some-one have bought this handy volume for you, you're going to feel a depth of gratitude towards that person. **But** that's **only** if you act on the advice contained within it.

A dear soul was visited regularly in her home, yet her condition continually worsened. One day, to the amazement of the doctor as well as the minister, she passed from this life. It was later discovered that her bedside drawer was full of unused prescriptions! Remedies were available - she need not have died, and, in a sense, she had no one to blame but herself. You **can** improve the quality of your life. But the proviso is that you not only ponder appropriate advice but that you practice it. To have merely acquired this book is insufficient: like the Christian gospel it needs to be appropriated and assimilated too.

CHAPTER X

FRESH IN THE MORNING; BRIGHT THROUGH THE DAY

How wonderful it is to awaken fresh at dawn and ready and willing to face the prospects and onslaughts of a new day! Regrettably, for so very many folk, the thoughts on awakening in the morning upon a weekday often given little incentive to rise. Yet the tiredness that afflicts so many of us on awakening is not so much the expression of the body as of the mind. The former has had the whole previous night in which to recuperate and build up reserves and this is the time when the physical frame should be full of bounce and ready for action! Indeed, here, as in many other spheres, it is the mind that dictates to the body and encourages it so often towards hibernation.

That physical factors do have their part to play in fatigue and listlessness is undoubtedly a fact, but it is equally a fact that by far the greatest percentage of all lethargy is basically situated within the mind. The analogy of fainting is a matter of consideration here. Though some folk faint because of physical disease or malfunction, it would nevertheless appear that the many who faint at the sight of blood, at confronting an unpleasant task, or at the shock of bad news do so at the dictate of the unconscious mind. They are mentally relieved of a literally unbearable confrontation. So, similarly, as the mind uses the body to avoid an unbearable burden by bringing about a faint, so, equally, the same mental process creates a preference for, and feeling conducive towards, sleep when unpleasantness confronts the mind at the beginning of a day.

65

That past conditioning over the years has been favourably conducive towards rising early is hardly the case! With what does the child usually associate arising in the morning? Most mornings it's in order to attend school, where, for several hours each day, the youngster is going to undergo discipline. Does not this go against the grain? Yes, of course it does! And what happens when schooldays are past and the experiences of youth have taken over? You've got it! More restrictions to be faced, when as a junior, one is bossed and bullied, and made a general muggins at the place where one has begun to sample work for the first time. In other words, if the mind is, at a subconscious level, going to use the body to get out of unpleasant situations then it is hardly likely to bring about a zestful spirit most mornings. The contrary is more likely the case and most of us experience it only too well. The will may be determined to arise, but the imagination concerning what the day is going to drag us through is sufficient to bring about lethargy, sloth and mental debility. And the latter is not to be castigated as mere shirking of responsibility! It is every bit as real and as crippling as a weak or underactive heart. Just as with the best lungs and heart in the world one can truly collapse, so with all the willpower in the world, one can find it an impossibility to throw off listlessness and lack of drive. Remember Cou'e's law of reversed effect!

Just as fainting is frequently an effect of psychological stress, one can equally affirm that fatigue, mental lethargy and debility are frequently tricks of the mind. Take for example the instance of a group of weary soldiers, worn out, supposedly in a physical capacity. They feel they can go no more than a few yards before they collapse. The journey has proved never-ending. In the scorch of the evening sun they feel so parched and ready to die through lack of water. Their hearts are beating heavily and their breathing is becoming more laboured. Indeed, they almost drag their feet forward. But then, all of a sudden and too good to be true, upon the horizon they not only see the glimmer of water, they also discover civilisation. Can they still go no further than several yards before they collapse? No, of course not. They yell and shout for all their worth with a deafening volume. And they **run** towards the destined goal!

A mother, similarly, may be completely whacked at the end of a busy day. But should her child be in difficulties, then, knowing of it, the mother remains awake for nights at a time to nurse her offspring.

Do you want another analogy? Well here it is, and it must suffice. Two apparently weak and lifeless folk are dawdling through a field, too tired to walk at a decent pace. But then, to their utter horror the sound of hoofs is heard galloping towards their rear. Looking round, they see a mad-eyed bull coming in their direction. Are they still physically incapacitated? The odds, as you realise is that they are not. A gate which normally they could never mount, on this occasion they jump with an unusual agility!

The above illustrations may well convey that all lethargy is within the psyche. Indeed, this is usually the case. Physical fatigue, however, **can** be the result of excessive hard work or undue exercise. Constant physical stress will undoubtedly create an excess of lactic acid within the bloodstream; and this will certainly bring about lethargy within the brain and nervous system. What I'm affirming is that this is hardly likely to be the case when a change of mental outlook results in a spurt of fresh energy. And it is certainly the least likely to be the cause when the body has awakened in the morning after having a full night to recuperate.

Tiredness is most frequently the mind's way of getting the conscious self out of unbearable situations; and perhaps the most frequent and most common of these is frustration or monotony. There is also lack of clarity or systematic functioning. We'll discuss them in turn.

Nothing saps the mind more than monotony or lack of

variation: it is, indeed, no surprise that more coronaries are brought about and experienced by those whose work is tedious or mentally trying than by those who are physically active.

Boredom comes under the same kind of category, for nothing is more tiring and exhausting than ennui! Is it to be wondered at, then, that so many newly retired people suffer from coronaries and a host of other killer diseases?

Concerning the mental exhaustion that afflicts the disorganised, it would appear that so much time is taken up directing the traffic of one's mind that one's state is comparable to that of a disorganised traffic warden on point duty, where the lights at a busy thoroughfare have broken down and he has created a chaotic mess and then retired from the scene completely shattered and exhausted. On the contrary, an experienced police patrol might then step into his shoes, keep the traffic moving in sequence, and retire later, still full of vim and vitality.

Your task is - with the things of the mind - to follow the example of the latter and **not** the former (and more about this in the next chapter).

See to it that you organise your daily timetable the way an efficient office clerk or company secretary deals with the mail she receives and distributes. This way, you'll find each new day filled with ordered opportunities and surprises. Each new day will be anticipated not only as a challenge, but as a challenge you will experience the joy of mastering. With that mastering there will be experienced the pleasure of triumph. Frustrations will diminish.

Yes, lethargy in the morning is most probably the outcome of years of conditioning. Deep down within the mind (to be discussed later), your other mental self has learned to associate early rising with unpleasant repercussions. The same mind cannot be reconditioned overnight, but with the passing of months and faithful adherence to the advice given in these pages, a new process of associations will build up, and with them a form of truly constructive reconditioning. Your mind is in the process of being wonderfully transformed and its happening quicker than you realise!

CHAPTER XI

ONE AT A TIME, PLEASE!

How often have we been about to board a coach when folk have been pushing from all sides, and the wise conductor or driver has had to shout out forcefully, 'Just one at a time please!' Indeed, the wisdom of such a request is discernable for any with a scrap of intelligence. For not only can the speediest way of entering a vehicle be accomplished by the one-at-a-time procedure, the reverse is also relevant: the speediest way of leaving a vehicle, or, indeed, a room, is by the one-at-a-time method. How many lives could have been spared had not folk panicked in a damaged plane or some other confined space and all converged on the exist at the same time!

A memory from far-off days comes to the mind of the writer - recollections of assisting mother with the hand mincer clamped to the kitchen table. I learned via trial and error that to cram too much produce all together into the funnel of the apparatus was merely to jam the mechanism. The gentle procedure was, indeed, the only one that worked successfully!

In more recent years, the coffee-grinder might well have a similar moral to teach us - cramming too much at the same time merely strains, and makes inactive, the mechanism and may well result in irreparable damage.

One more analogy has surely a lesson to teach us here. It is the example of the egg-timer. So designed is this contraption that the narrowness of the neck only permits a minimum of sand to pass through at any given time. Your time must be comparable to that egg timer's small neck.

One by one the sands are flowing,
One by one the moments fall;
Some are coming, some are going;
Do not strive to grasp them all.

One by one thy duties wait thee;
Let thy whole strength go to each;
For, though future dreams elate thee,
Learn thou first what these can teach.
(A.A.Procter)

All these analogies quoted in the above paragraph are surely sufficient in themselves to show us the error of much of our past with relation to how we organised our time. Indeed, a more appropriate term would be 'disorganised it!' For example, you probably rise in the morning, and if the postman has been good and the mail is abundant, then you tear open those envelopes, scatter the contents everywhere; pick out the letters that inspire you and, as for those bills or letters that require tedious replies your mind has a wonderful way of allowing them to get temporarily displaced! But regrettably for you, the senders haven't forgotten their contents even if you have! Soon you are quite likely to find yourself in embarrassing circumstances: letters have been ignored by you which should have received attention; and bills should have been paid. It's not much compensation paying them once the electricity has been cut off or the telephone disconnected! Indeed, a reconnection charge plus inability to receive urgent calls is the kind of price to be paid over and above what should have been competently transacted but wasn't. This because you allowed the mind to be swamped, first thing, by an abundance of mail which you attended to in liquorice all-sorts fashion: picking out the ones you liked and discarding the remainder!

Surely a much more sensible approach regarding factors such as one's daily mail is to see to each letter immediately. Admittedly, a truly urgent letter deserves first priority but as for all that follow, a mixed diet is often far better to cope with than to enjoy all the goodies while hoarding up a collection of hard nuts for the morrow!

The morrow - a convenient term, isn't it? "Don't bother to do this today; there is always tomorrow!" There was once a pub in Shropshire which advertised above the bar, 'Free drinks here tomorrow'. Well, the folk turned up on the morrow, and on their request for a free pint or two the publican merely said with a smile, "Can't you read it? It says free drinks tomorrow!" The moral is, of course, that in a very real sense tomorrow never arrives; only the day after. To put off till tomorrow what can be done today is, therefore, usually quite an unwise policy. Though there are but twenty four hours in any particular day - and time **must** be given for relaxation and sleep - we must not allow our responsibilities to pile up. Such piles may be pushed out of our consciousness, and appear as 'Out of sight, then out of mind!' But their weight is still there, and deep down the subconscious knows all about them and is bearing the strain.

Days then, just like hours, are to be faced one at a time. It's no use allowing past days of remorse to demobilise the present (They've taught us their lessons - at least they should have done! We can use their memory as assets). Our task is to live for today. For the present alone is actual reality. Yesterday is no more than a memory; and as for tomorrow, it is no more than a possibility if the good Lord spares us! We owe it to ourselves to concentrate and focus our energies on transforming reality rather than fretting or fuming about the past or worrying ourselves about the unforeseen future. This is not to say that we shouldn't prepare ourselves for future events. Indeed, we most certainly should! The fact is that we mustn't use up energy in brooding over the future which can be used constructively to make the present secure and stable. In a very real sense, today well spent is a safeguard for the day after. In the Bible, Jesus is purported to have said, 'Take no thought for the morrow. Sufficient unto the day is the evil thereof'. (*Matthew 6:34*) The truth is that the meaning of language often changes with the passing of the centuries. And just as charity is no longer identical with love, (*1 Corinthians 13:13*) so, similarly, the term 'take no thought' is translated in all reliable up-to-date Bible translations as 'Be not anxious' or 'do not worry'.

To use mental discipline and, shall we say, departmentalise our time and activities is something we must truly master to live life fully. The most charismatic men and women have learned to do this very thing! The Prime Minister is not as physically robust as possibly the athlete who has bought the corner shop. The latter possibly frets and fumes because a group of customers come to be served while a traveller has called and a delivery van arrives. He might well have difficulty in coping with such a situation. And when it's over and he is able to 'lock up shop' and get home, he probably flops exhausted and feels he has had an exceedingly hectic day. But consider our Prime Minister and what he has got to get through in a normal working day. Yet at the end of it he is most probably still very calm and serene. The simple fact is that he knows how to use his mind to organise his timetable, while the poor shopkeeper with all his physical strength, just doesn't.

You, dear reader, **must** organise your time - indeed, a diary can prove very helpful here, as can a tray for incoming and outgoing correspondence. And as a reward, you will start to feel a sense of achievement which will spur you yet further. You will get through your commitments, not by choosing the soft raisins and accumulating the hard nuts, but by a daily diet of truly varied activity, the raisins helping you to digest the nuts!

One thing must certainly be stressed here and it is that 'all work and no play makes Jack a dull boy'. It is imperative that in mentally

73

departmentalising your time you learn to switch your mind off work for periods of relaxation. Should you constantly be bringing your troubles from work back into your home then it is because you have not developed, sufficiently the art of mental departmentalism. It has been said of Winston Churchill that he was able to switch his mind off meetings with the war cabinet, enter his studio and get so enthralled with his paints as to be temporarily oblivious to all else. And indeed, in a not unsimilar sense, a like quality was apparent in Archbishop William Temple, who temporarily gave himself so completely to those whom he interviewed that they felt he had no other interest in the whole world except the problem on which they'd sought his advice.

In work, then, as in play, be master of your mind. Learn the art of departmentalism; and though, as in all things new, difficulties will usually be encountered, practice alone will make perfect. Rome wasn't built in a day; but each victory will spur you that bit higher. So remember: one thing at a time, one day at a time. And when you arrive at the end of this book and begin to put into practice that which you have learnt, it will be well, indeed, if you recap by giving priority to the contents of one chapter at a time.

CHAPTER XII

A VIEW FROM THE HEIGHTS

Behind a Colne Valley church in Yorkshire was a steep winding lane, and from the top of it the writer felt transported at night into another world. Ascending the slope in the evening air he left the closeness of human intercourse, and, breathing in the cool air of the night, was transported into an atmosphere of intense peace and stillness. From reaching one of several spots along the plateau, the view to be held across the valley was quite marvellous. The stars glittering in the sky above, were complemented by those lesser lights below; and many of the lesser lights conveyed their own message for they were a reminder of the occupants of certain homes, one or two of whom may have been very nasty, but thankfully many more were extremely nice. He thought of that massive multitude of souls, within that large valley; of the marvel of a God who's all searching eye constantly watched over them; and yet, possibly only a smattering of children and old folk would have an eye for Him!

A wonderful occasion this view from a summit; one the author wouldn't have missed for the world. Yes, it proved a temporary relief to get away from the involvement of living to the contemplation of it. To separate oneself from it for but a brief period was to view it from a worthwhile perspective. One could later resume one's tasks in a sane and balanced manner.

Let me give you an analogy of the above which concerned a one and only trip to Paris. There the writer watched an artist who intrigued him; a Frenchman who appeared emotional and not a little

75

dissatisfied because of the work he was undergoing using canvas and oils. Every now and again this little Frenchman would begin to peer and squint at the work with which he was in close proximity. Then he would stop, take a pace or two back, gesticulate with arms and shoulders, weigh and consider and then smile. Yes, he knew what next to do and with a happy countenance resumed his work at close quarters. It was this stepping back process that made all the difference, for without it his eyes would have become so blurred and the completed work would have made little sense.

If our daily life is to have sense and meaning then it must be viewed by us from a right perspective. We must give ourselves occasions for stepping apart; and if the stepping apart can be upwards too then we will doubly benefit. The Christian knows that though he must labour below that his citizenship is in Heaven. Like the street artist we need to keep our visionary muscles alternating between close and distant proximities. Eye muscle exercises are good for the spirit as well as for the body as the late Dr. Bates of 'Better Eyes Without Glasses' would have well and truly endorsed! Blurred vision comes through too much close work and puts everything out of perspective; see that you strengthen your eyes by equally using them for distance. There are far too many people with whom we rub shoulders whose existence is puny because their world is myopic. So wrapped up are they with their own little world that their little things appear as large, and tiny grievances are viewed as titanic grudges.

Myopic living is a disease which causes others to suffer too. Scrooge, who viewed his miserly world as the only one, entertained a subconscious suspicion that Bob Cratchit was getting more out of life than he, even though Scrooge had all the money and poor Bob had hardly any! This led Scrooge to take things out on Bob and upon all others who smiled for some reason. And Scrooge's attitude still prevails amongst those who are wrapped in their own puny existence yet perceive others outside of it enjoying themselves.

It is strange, yet understandable, that many whose life styles are high, responsibility and status great, have a secret envy towards those whose life styles are far less demanding. A certain mill manager, and a director too, resigned his post to secure that of a menial employee elsewhere where the wage was less but then, so was the responsibility. The man's health rapidly improved, and so, indirectly did that of his family! Whatever qualities the man lacked, at least, he had his priorities right: health before wealth and peace before prestige! Incidentally, at least two others of the directorship hinted to the writer that they could have followed their colleague's example, but loss of pride to their families as well as to themselves deterred them from acting. Yes it would appear that the grass constantly appears greener on the other side of the fence. However, not a few who go over find that it's remarkably, quite bitter. 'I have learned in whatever state I am therewith to be satisfied', (*Philippians 4:11*)wrote a New Testament apostle, and this is not to be confused with a Godly ambition which spurred him on whenever the right opportunity presented itself

For sanities sake, if for nothing else, each individual needs to get away from daily occupational hazards, **not** so as to abandon them but to re-evaluate them in a true dimension. Ascending the steep gradient behind the churchyard on a day when a traffic congestion obstructed the main road which ran along the bottom, the writer left the din from noisy horns and cursing drivers to the ripple of a spring and the singing of the birds. Soon he was looking along the valley from above. He could see the cause of the pile up; a large tanker being pulled to the side of the road by a crane; and the police patrol was already motioning the first flow of traffic to resume.

If only those frustrated drivers at the foot of the hill could have been temporarily elevated to the top and back, they would have ceased from fuming and fretting. They would have known that, considering the circumstances, things were in control. Yes, situations that could so easily boil over and do damage can be turned low through a view from the plateau.

When did you last get on those hiking shoes and possibly climb to the top of a hill? When did you last look down upon life, viewing the valley or plain below and possibly the heights beyond? Perhaps the valleys are the most foreboding! Realise this however, that for every valley encountered in life there must be, at least, two hills or plateaux. You can't have a valley without hills: one at each side! It's one of the blessed compensations of life, and many of those Yorkshire towns and cities once known for grimy mills, warehouses and back to back dwellings were more than compensated for by the grandeur and glory of the many hills or plateaux which joined to encircle a crater of smoke and smog. It was as if nature was endeavouring to offer its own compensation towards those whose existence from dawn to dusk was fettered (yes, for youngsters it was once literally, to spinning frames or looms!)

However, my emphasizing was on footwear, and the need to hike! Yes, one cannot emphasise enough the need to protect the body by care and exercise. Indeed, the man who neglects to care for his body is an utter fool. He'll never be given another. He might be given several marriages, homes and cars. He **might** be given a second chance just as the antediluvians were within the very Bible itself, by Our Lord (*1 Peter 3:19-20*). But as for a second body in this life- Not a chance! He who abuses or mishandles it is a fool indeed.

For those who equate their theology with the New Testament the body is to be viewed as a habitation occupied by two: the conscious self and the conquering Christ! It is a humbling and an awesome thought. It is a stupendous claim for any one to make but it is nevertheless, for the Christian the clear teaching of the Word of God (*1 Corinthians 3:16-17*).

Always remember too, that normally the hikers, sun worshippers, athletes and joggers, are a much more radiant and serene type than are the bingo criers and the booze consumers. It's purely a matter of how part of our marvellous mechanism interacts upon another.

To keep the body in trim many seem to take things by leaps and bounds rather than by steps and limits, and this is the chief criticism of so many who practice jogging. The exercise is certainly beneficial, but only on the proviso that it is never overdone. Alas, we are often too impetuous and we would do well to increase our paces and our distances 'slow but sure'. Because of erraticism this beneficial sport receives more publicity through misuse than use. Cycling also has much to commend it and the writer visited a lady who fell off hers at sixty-five. She was determined to re-commence on being released from hospital. Need one wonder that she looked no more than forty-five! Yes, most pastimes and outdoor pursuits need not be limited to any age group and, though a whole host more could be commended, I'm sure Father Time has amply shown that Mother Nature commends walking, up hill, down dale, or on the level more than all; and like most of the best things in life, including the Christian Gospel itself (*Romans 6:23 & 4:5*) it is entirely free.

Walking up a hill at a sensible pace serves two purposes. We not only receive exercise for the body but enlightenment for the mind; and this is not always the case while exercising oneself along a low stretch of plain. By coming apart from the oftimes mundane through ascending the slopes we learn to look down at what we temporarily leave behind. But first we alter our focus from the short distances into the long - gradually and subconsciously. We're diverted from the warring plain below because our eyes are directed up the slope. The ascent already affects our bodily posture, we lift our head high and this has a reflex effect upon our very mind and spirit. It is the raised head that is associated with courage, openness and straight dealing; a contrast indeed to a lowered head which triggers off to the subconscious associations and feelings of discouragement, despair, despondency and defeat.

The only time the ascent of a hill determines the droop of the head is when one temporarily stops to turn back and view the progress one has made. The rational mind often makes this an excuse when actually the real motive is need for a rest, as one is now not quite as young! The look, however, is followed by surprise at the progress one has already made. The work of transformation has already begun. Often a lot in a very short while! Need one wonder that the sweet singer of Israel could sing, 'I to the hills will lift my eyes, from whence commeth my help'. (*Psalm 121:1*) Yes, the temporary glance back is in looking towards the gloom and turmoil one has separated oneself from so as to revitalise the life force within. The backward glance, however, is hardly to be commended (*Luke 9:62*); it has resulted in many a tragedy (*Genesis 19:26*). 'Come away', not 'Look back' is the cry of the uplands.

The writer used to make his regular evening climb by first of all having to traverse a wild and often overgrown churchyard. He passed through the region of the dead before he could start the ascent; and is it not true that before any of us can ascend the heights of the aesthetically transforming that we need to have sampled the low region of the aesthetically and spiritually inanimate? Death must be seen to appreciate life. One will rarely find spiritual life in the region of the mills and workshops, the turmoil, friction and traffic of a materialistic existence. Those roses that do occasionally grow amongst the smoke, smog and scrapheaps of such sordid scenes are rare gems indeed. As rare as the gold amongst the grit of the mine their existence is the exception rather than the rule.

Yes, the 'dead centre' of that past Parish was, for the writer, not only a reminder of the need to climb above and beyond the spiritually dead in order to raise one's spirits, it also became a reminder that one had no real desire to change places with the literal dead! The promises given by religion concerning a hereafter might be yea and amen; hymns centred round life in the Glory Land may be infinite. But even the devout are seldom keen to make a premature take off!

"Live daily at the grave's mouth, Die daily, Prepare for eternity!" wrote the first Incumbent within the first copy of the Parish's magazine. A sombre thought, indeed, one might think. Yet is not that the message of the cemetery? 'Make the most of life while you have it. Time is short and eternity long!'

Working amongst the deprived children of London's East End a delightful lady had to travel on a tube which took her to the school of which she was a head. The train passed a large bleak cemetery. "Some mornings I think my life is dreary, meaningless, and it's such an effort to face another day with unruly kids," she said, "but then I look at that cemetery and I wonder how many of the occupants would prefer to change place with me, and I count my blessings, thank my God for another day and rejoice at being alive and privileged to teach." Helen's lesson can be ours too!

Thankfully we can rise well above the domain of the dead and breathe the life giving vitality of the hills. We can perch ourselves on life's plateau and, being on top of the world, as it were, adjust from shortsightedness to longsightedness and it becomes an eye salve for body and soul alike. Here we can choose to identify ourselves with the gods above Olympus if not with Christ on Olivet. One can look downwards towards the thriving community below which is still busily fretting itself over apparent nonentities. And we view it no longer as a slave fettered to it but as a King from a castle, or a Queen from a throne; perhaps as the Grecian Pantheon looked down upon earthly mortals with scorn if not for sport; please God, as Jesus looked towards Jerusalem and wept over it! (*Luke 19:41*)

The Nazarene was one who constantly retired to the mountains. It was the late James Stalker who once commented, 'As others on reaching a city might ask the quickest way to the best hotel He would have asked for the quickest way to the nearest mountain!' He sought such raised regions in order that He might thrash out His future works plan with His Father's guidance before choosing the apostleship; (*Luke 6: 12 & 13*) He chose it after his nearest and closest earthly friends misunderstood His teaching; and from the slopes He received not only the assurance of a Father in Heaven but the close presence of loved ones who had left their earthly sojourn years previous (*Luke 9:30 & 31*).

The reader can learn from above; from the heights he may be assured that loved ones who left our fleshly existence many years previous are nearer than previously realised. On the plateau one might recollect anew the advice and comfort that loved ones gave in far off days. Those who helped us through those years of infancy as well as the slippery paths of youth can become very real again. Those voices can, as it were, speak to you as they have to countless others who picnic on those picturesque plateaux of life's opportunities. The dear and holy dead are **not** the prerogative of the clairvoyant, the Spiritualist and the eerie seance (*Isaiah 8:19*). They are part of the historic churches teaching. It concerns a communion of saints which, alas, religious folk witness to weekly in their creed but hardly ever witness to in their lives! The only saints most of them seem to know about is that questionable line whom previous pontiffs, starting with John XV canonized and a recent one, John XXIII chose to shorten.

Sainthood in the New Testament is the possession of every humble believer (*e.g. 2 Corinthians 1:1; Ephesians 1:1*); and those believers parted from us in the flesh are very much alive in the spirit. They encircle us daily as we fight the good fight in life's arena (*Hebrews 12:1*). Their voices are joined with God in spurring us on; but we can only hear them again if we will come apart from the din which deafens and the existence that seeks to destroy us. We need the separateness and the silence of the heights.

In George Bernard Shaw's play, 'St. Joan' there is a conversation between the Dauphin of France and Joan of Arc. The latter says she has heard voices that come from the heavens, advising her what to do. The leader of France becomes annoyed: "Why don't they come to me; I'm the king, not you!" Joan simply replies to him, "They do come to you, but you do not hear them. You have not sat in the field in the evening listening for them. When the angelus rings you merely cross yourself and you have done with it: but if you prayed **with your heart,** and listened to the thrilling of the bells in the air, after they stop ringing you would hear the voices as well as I do."

Yes, reader the voices are still there but you've got to come apart to hear them. The very hills may be alive with the sound of music, but with a Julie Andrews you've to climb them if you are to hear it!

From the heights communion is made, and things considered once dead and mute become alive again. From those grandiose heights one breathes the air of Heaven; the plan and purpose of our pilgrimage unfolds; and assurance of the good land beyond the present one gives us the ability to descend to the plains **and the valleys.** Yes, no longer to be their victim but their victor; no longer as conquered but as conqueror!

Alas, practical compliance not just poetic contemplation is required of the reader. This **can** be a problem: because the hill regions in many parts are hardly fit for the fairer sex to traverse unaccompanied. 'Do gooders' have created for us a sick society indeed where villains suffer less as victims suffer more. Women are hardly safe in daylight never mind the dark! Let that evening stroll apart then, be in the company of man's greatest friend: a four legged pal whose faithfulness is possibly much more staunch than that of many humans. Such a creature will by no means rob you of your spiritual nourishment from the slopes; dumb creatures are often more sensitive to spiritual presences than we are (*Numbers 22:33*); and I don't think dogs are any less so than donkeys. We envisage a puny spirit world indeed, if its only occupants are geriatric humans!

The writer has given homes to poor abandoned mongrels and moggies through the years. Rescued dogs have proved the healthiest and most grateful of creatures. He has never once regretted it; his only regret is that others fail to understand the solace, the joy and the comfort these beautiful creatures are able to impart. It's as if another dimension for living is totally lacking from their lives. Let those who are lonely unfulfilled or afraid realise that the answer no doubt rests at their feet!

CHAPTER XIII

CALM IN THE MIDST OF THE STORM

The disciples of the Galilean were once caught in a ferocious storm (*Matthew 8:23-26*). It disturbed them deeply that their Master was able to sleep through the midst of it; they awoke Him to ask whether He cared not that they might all perish. Nothing as infectious as panic, yet Jesus didn't seem at all ruffled. He immediately rebuked the wind; a great calm followed, and He simply questioned them about their lack of faith.

There's always a feeling of elation when a calm takes the place of a storm; the air is always fresh, the leaves on land are moist and mother nature appears to be alive again, humming with activity. Why, the whole of creation once the storm is over seems one with us as we walk along the highways breathing the freshness and witnessing the sparkle of living. Before long the sun might well follow, and if it does then the appearance of a rainbow - God's covenant with the whole of life (*Genesis 9: 9-17*) - may make its presence as real to the eye as the atmosphere has permeated both ear and nostril. Yes, the experience of peace after storm is most welcome: a stillness and serenity which supersedes tension, if not turmoil. It clears one's head and lifts up the drooping spirit.

Our materialistic plane equally benefits when a long awaited peace suddenly supersedes strife as when songs of victory supersede shells of violence. Older folk remember how their spirits knew no limit once V.E.Day was declared, and V.J.Day proved similar. The conductor never bothered to collect his fares; the cinema offered its free performances; and many a publican would not realise the price of **his** generosity until the next morning! But who couldn't rejoice when loved ones would now be returning home, and songs made famous by the forces sweetheart (Vera Lynn) would be actualised?

The above was a wonderful manifestation of peace; yet others might experience a vastly different form when the exam room is vacated, the scratching of pens has ceased, and one goes out into the open realising one has done one's best. The results may not be known for quite some weeks to follow; but - for now, at least the text books are closed and one can shout 'yippee!'

Yes, in so many diverse ways one knows what it is to relax after the turmoil and participate in an almost supernatural ecstasy which follows: think of a young mother who has just given birth to a wonderful little bundle of life. The labour and the fear is passed and already, perhaps, forgotten because of something wonderful that has arrived.

But is not the departure sometimes as hallowed as one's arrival into this world? Is it not often similar when a lovely creature breathes his or her last breath? A silence seems to have fallen upon the spot as if an angel of death has just fluttered in to take a loved one into a far more glorious sphere. The shell of this life's limitations has had to be broken that the life within might learn to use its wings, its vision and its voice! The dark, cramped womb of this world has been vacated. Liberation has come to the captive! The labourers work is over; death conveys its own dignity. Yes, and even when in human reckoning it seems to be so unfairly premature, for those who have the previous gift of faith there is a peace and serenity in what follows: Yes, as placid and beautiful as any Easter garden, where the Messiah was laid after being 'cut down' in the very midst of years Himself!

"Go home content, the evening falls,
Day's tired sinews are unbent;
No more the thrush or linnet calls,
The twilight fades, go home content."

"Father, the field is but half-turned,
And yet the spring is well-nigh spent."
"My son, the hour of rest is earned,
The day's work done, go home content."
(Anon.)

As for babes and infants, why they're too good, one often feels, for this corrupting world; but for those who have carried such a life merely to see it taken away, the cross must be heavy indeed. Blest, indeed, are those who have a plot in which to remember it even though it become one's weekly Gethsemane. That is, until a possible bulldozer obliterates the cemetery, for the dead are no more respected now than are the living! Dear bereft mother, remember one thing: you now have a unique gift in comforting others who enter your Gethsemane. You are **not** alone. Others must also traverse your path. But do not weep perpetually for your offspring. 'For of such is the Kingdom of Heaven'. The streets of the New Jerusalem are full of little children playing in them. Yes, and surely pets too!

Older children, of course, have forged yet a closer attachment because of the years shared together. Their decease appears yet more tragic still. Yet they often accomplish in nine years what others fail to do in ninety. One little fellow, on temporarily parting from his pets, pals and parents said, "Mummy, I can see the angels - they're coming for me now!" and, of course, to any soulless sceptic of a professor one had only to say: "Look at the little boy's face. The confirmation is there. Why, it's shining like the sun. Would that your face was the same!"

The storms and turmoils of living affect us all on this sphere and sometimes they come upon us so unexpectedly. One moment all in life is going well, but then - when we least expect it - a cloud-burst envelops us and we're fortunate indeed if we can find a speedy refuge.

In Babbington Coombe one can still enter a little cave which a Victorian clergyman once sheltered in when, one bright sunny afternoon, the weather suddenly changed, as we commonly say, for the worst! But what a blessing came from such an incident. The thunder growled above, the lightning flashed before his eyes, the rain descended in torrents; yet the frail Vicar was secure within that cleft of a rock. And his mind went back to biblical days, and to others who'd found refuge from the shelter of a rock. Then spying a playing card on the ground of the small cavern, he took it up and was inspired to write on the back of it words which countless numbers have ever since used as a hymn: 'Rock of Ages'. Yes, but for that storm and Augustus Toplady finding a place of refuge; but for that card found on the floor; Christian hymn books would have been short of one that has been a solace to millions.

Each storm in life serves its purpose: "I'm glad I came in here from the wet Vicar, what a lovely Church this is and it has such a delightful atmosphere. I've never been in here before though I've past it almost every day!" Yes, a storm in the Colne Valley had served its purpose and that young lady, with her child, became spiritually enriched!

The title of this chapter, however, is not one of peace after the storm or of peace from the storm, but that of peace within it! It is the peace which the Galilean alone experienced in the boat while the storms raged on Genasaret's Lake and the water began to enter the vessel. It is the message of **inner** serenity, of a peace from which the external gales of life can never rob us. Such a situation may be aptly given from a scene the writer beheld amidst the roar of a heavy waterfall within beautiful Wales. The scene was most glorious even though quite deafening to the ear; for though the water poured down those rocks like an avalanche, there, to one side - perched on a rock was a tiny bird. It kept looking up and gave a chirp, yes, even though the foam was at the base of the rock through the speed of water descending and rushing around it with such great force. The little creature showed little if any concern for the roar and force of the waters; I think it knew itself to be resting on a secure foundation! Was not that little creature singing in the midst of, what must have been for it a veritable storm? What that bird could do, you, the reader can also do!

The England of Wesley's day was actually more crooked, corrupt and certainly far more religious than today. While the religious establishment flourished, and Vicars were frequently the epitome of hypocrisy the materially less privileged could drown their sorrows by getting drunk for a half-penny, blind drunk for a penny; and for two pence they could have straw provided as well! Wesley and others realised that such permissiveness led to perniciousness and that license given to the wealthy was often at the cost of enslaving the poor. Destined for so-called holy orders this aspiring little man from Epworth - never feel inferior if you are small of stature, Wesley was only 5ft. 3ins.! - sought to reform the Nation's moral level. He subsequently formed a holy club in Oxford and the regulations enforced a methodical pattern of morality.

The term Methodist dated from such a venture, being first used in derision, and Wesley after ordination sought to further its practice much further afield. Indeed, he would even consider introducing such strictures to the new colonies; well, at least he would seek to enforce it in far off Georgia where he arrived as a missionary priest. Alas, after less than two years the aspiring 'little man' was on the return journey feeling that his journey had been a total waste of time. "I went to America to convert the Indians" he affirmed: "But who shall convert me?"

What had caused such an outburst from this young missionary

whose life had been so governed by a methodical religious discipline? Primarily the fact that during a ferocious storm on the voyage out to Georgia he became as terrified as the worst worldling when caught in the grip of an unexpected storm. He felt that his life was as insecure as the rest on that terrifying journey. Well, all except a group of missionaries from Moravia! These were indeed a unique exception. The ship was rolling as well as rocking. Any moment it would seem as if the strain would be too much for the vessel and a watery grave seemed imminent for all. Yet, wonder of wonders, this little band of Moravians were actually singing in the midst of it all.

The little man from Epworth couldn't cease to be amazed at the radiance and serenity of this happy group who remained so calm and complacent. Like that little bird in Wales these too sang while billows assailed. They could sing because they believed they were resting on a sure foundation, Christ, the rock of ages! Years were to pass and that same sense of calm in the midst of commotion would become an every day experience with the little man himself. Wesley would later be repeatedly encircled by mobs out to beat the living daylights out of this firebrand for God. He would be hounded by thugs employed by profligate vicars. On one occasion a notorious high-wayman would threaten the minister with his life, but this little man had become a spiritual giant and was so relaxed in the storms himself that He emulated his Lord's serenity in the tempest on Lake Galilee. Casting his purse to the highwayman he said: "The time will come when you will have cause to regret your manner of living. When it does just remember these words: 'The blood of Jesus Christ, God's Son, cleanseth from all sin'. Now pray, have me excused." Wesley pursued his journey, and that day the Highwayman was converted.

This serenity in the midst of storm, this calmness in the midst of chaos can be experienced as much by you today as it has been by men of faith and integrity down the centuries, and by none so much as by the Man from Nazareth Himself. One needn't be a Christian to appreciate such qualities. Pilate, the sceptic, uttered no truer words than when he uttered, 'Behold, The Man!' (*John 19:5*). Those conversant with Holy Week narrative might remember how Jesus was tried and tortured through the accusations of the religious elite, how He was jeered at by the crowds, how He was ridiculed by the soldiers, how He brought tension, conflict and chaos amongst His opponents.

The chief priests of Judaism - the epitome of Jewish Nationalism - cries out, "We have no king but Caesar!" (*John 19:15*). The supreme judge of the land says, "I am innocent of the blood of this just person," (*Matthew 27:24*), yet has him scourged and turned over to the mob. Yes, Pilate was dumbfounded at the calmness of his prisoner. He'd tried to get the prisoner to defend Himself. "Knowest thou not that I have power to crucify thee or release thee?" he affirms. But the prisoner merely said in a calmness that utterly baffles, "Thou could'st have no power - - except it were given thee from above!" (*John 19:10-11*). Remember Rudyard Kipling's words: "If you can keep your head when all around are losing theirs and blaming it on you? If you can trust yourself when all men doubt you, yet make allowance for their doubting too! - - If you can bear to hear the truth you've spoken twisted by knaves to make a trap for fools!" Yes, if anyone fulfilled Kipling's great lines centuries before they were penned the Nazarene did. And what He Himself fulfilled He expected His followers to do.

Indeed, for those who have the faith to believe it, the Nazarene is still close at hand, and they who take Him into their barque will laugh at every storm! It is the writer's contention that He has the whole world in His hand and yet paradoxically He comes to dwell in the lowly heart. All that's required is that He be sincerely invited (*Revelation 3:20*). His real temple is neither a building or a tabernacle but the heart of a humble believer, (*Acts 7:48*) and none more so than the heart of a little child! (*Matthew 18:5*)

Yes, indeed, Divine guidance is *not* dependent upon the ability to read and accept a denominational creed. It is knowing the Christ of the creed that counts. It has been the writer's experience over the years to discover that often the mentally retarded, as well as the least privileged materially, are often the most advanced spiritually. The writer's youngest son, James, was mentally damaged at an early age through too much oxygen being administered to him while in a hospital, and, when he was ten years older, on visiting a fairground, he could hardly wait to have a go on the Noah's Ark! The ride was slower than usual as many children were aboard, nevertheless a trifle too fast for James's unsteady feet. As a consequence he fell to the revolving platform between the wooden animals, while all others - particularly adults - either didn't notice, or what was more obvious - just didn't want to know. But then, rushing across from the other side of the revolving merry-go-round, a fellow in his late teens or early twenties made a beeline to the spot. By this time the ride was slowing down and the one who had come to our little lad's aid had lifted him up, rubbed his poorly back and was repeatedly asking him if he was alright. Yes, James's rescuer was wearing, quite awkwardly, a ten gallon type of seaside hat; he had replaced a straw back into his mouth (or was it an imitation of a lengthy cigarette?) One thing **was** sure, a caring affinity was manifested from one retarded creature to another at a depth seldom expressed between the seemingly normal.

Yes, one learns to appreciate over the years that for each affliction in life there is a compensation. One, however, does not always appreciate it at the time. To see the retarded subnormal frequently abused by the considered normal can be a harrowing and soul destroying plight. The author is **still** haunted by a group of 'normal' children who danced round young James, jeering and taunting, while, in bewilderment and quietness, which lasted sometime after, this little boy began to realise inwardly that, somehow, he wasn't made the same as they. Yes, and what a Gethsemane for a dedicated mother to have beheld! Gethsemanes are **not** confined to the One that many in the Christian religion term 'The Son of God!' Dedicated Asian mothers experience such Gethsemanes each day within the third world while their little bundles of love breathe their last breath. The Divine, who alone can comfort at such a time is no more confined to a religion than some once considered Him confined to a little safe on an altar, called a tabernacle.

Friends, if these words are relevant in any way to you, then be assured that nature seeks to correct the imbalances of life. You, yourself, grieve over the imbalances of living; the injustice of so much. Have you not stopped to realise that He, who placed within you this quest for justice must believe in it Himself? Is it not feasible to believe that the justice which you support as a finite creature is but a gift from the Infinite - whoever you care to call Him? Does not your intelligence tell you that if justice is not transacted here then it needs to be transacted hereafter? O yes! life here seems, so often, so very unjust. But tell me, would you judge 'a play with a moral' when the curtain falls at the end of act one? Of course not! Then, why not have the common sense to believe that before the curtain falls at the final act in the hereafter that justice and love will have been perfectly expressed?

As for the present interim sojourn, be assured that the darkest hour comes before the dawn; while the darker the sky the brighter become those stars in the midst of it! And, to those who can accept it, many of these stars can become equivalent to you of what my fourth child, Andrew and sixth child, James, are to me: stars to guide one nearer to God. Your handicapped or deceased, possibly victims of iatrongenic disease or medical negligence[1], need not be **for you** a burden promoting a disruptive chaos but, please God, a blessing permeating a Divine calm.

(1) The writer's child, Andrew, died because the oxygen supply was accidently broken.

CHAPTER XIV

RECOGNISING DIMENSION AND DEPTH

The writer well remembers returning as a nineteen year old, fresh from a Bible College, conceited and cock sure. The Sunday that followed saw him seeking solitude on a bench while preparing a sermon for a service in a Baptist Church that was to follow. On that gorgeous afternoon, who made his way along that road but Old Norbury, a kind of recluse, from the workhouse on the opposite side of the road. The writer had viewed him approaching and lowered his head so as to meditate on the good book! The dear inmate, however, was not to be easily put off: 'I see you are reading the Bible," he said; while the writer considered that such a remark and intrusion was uncalled for. The poor fellow was not the cleanest of sights for, although he was dressed in the traditional rough haired cloth of the workhouses' residents, a well fitted suit, he was salivating profusely. The dear man had known much better days and some affirmed that too much study had been the factor which had triggered off such mental deterioration. The man now spoke through black stubs of teeth, yet his eyes glistened and, indeed, almost wept for joy as he began to say, "God is love you know!" Then he admonished the writer to look across at the trees and at the wild flowers: "God is love and He is everywhere; He is in the grass, the sky and the fields!" Then he pointed to himself, and with tears now pouring down his cheeks for gratitude, he said "And God is in me." He then arose and went on his way repeating, "Yes, God is in me!" and his eyes shone with a shekinah brilliance. The writer had been preparing a sermon on the a.b.c. of how to find Christ and get saved! He tore it up and realized that he still had a great deal to learn about Jesus which no institute would ever be able to impart. Some day the writer will look out for Old Norbury; he'll hope to push past Moses, Elijah and others and hug that dear old man who on that Sunday afternoon taught him so much!

Yes, indeed, just as the intensity of the evening darkness increases the brightness of the stars in the heavens, so similarly the greater the conflict on earth the more pronounced become heavenly characters around, if not for the spiritually perceptive the very Deity Himself! (*2 Kings 6:17*). The wonderful mystic Francis Thompson who lived in the end of the last century experienced much loneliness, sickness and poverty. He spent many nights on the Thames embankments as well as happier times at Charing Cross. His early despair and disillusionment became more than compensated for by a spiritual world into whose dimension the materialist knows nothing, but the worlds rejected and despised can know a great deal. After his death at forty-six this unfinished poem was found in his few possessions:

> *O World invisible, we view thee,*
> *O World intangible, we touch thee,*
> *O World unknowable, we know thee,*
> *Inapprehensible, we clutch thee!*
>
> *Does the fish soar to find the ocean,*
> *The eagle plunge to find the air -*
> *That we ask of the stars in motion*
> *If they have rumour of thee there?*

Not where the wheeling systems darken,
And our benumbed conceiving soars! -
The drift of pinions, would be hearken,
Beats at our own clay-shuttered doors.

The angels keep their ancient places; -
Turn but a stone, and start a wing!
'Tis ye, 'tis your estranged faces,
That miss the many-spendoured thing.

But (when so sad thou canst no sadder)
Cry; - and upon they so sore loss
Shall shine the traffic of Jacob's ladder
Pitched betwixt Heaven and Charing Cross.

Yea, in the night, my Soul, my daughter,
Cry, - clinging heaven by the hems;
And lo, Christ walking on the water,
Not of Genesareth, but Thames!

Dear reader, it is through our rejection by a harsh materialistic plane that we find acceptance into a world of a far deeper dimension. It is through the fire that the gold is purified; and though affliction will cause many to fall, to the one who has swapped life's heavy problems for its challenges every experience at the deep end, which might cause others to sink, will cause You to swim. The only weights that will become attached to your life will be analogous to what wings are to a bird; an unrecognised attachment for soaring. See that you use them!

Peace is a wonderful thing; if you have all the wealth that money can buy but do not possess peace then you are impoverished indeed; like General Naaman who became a leper, not the poorest slave in Syria would want to swap places with you! (*2 Kings 5:1*). There are many of this world's affluent who, though they be envied by others, are secretly unable to rest because of a nagging conscience more persistent and painful than an abscessed tooth. Regrettably, while they know of the remedy for the latter they are ignorant of the needed therapy for the former. In this drug orientated society the conscience deadener becomes too often equated with the sleeping pill. They fail to realise that what they can shut off from the surface of their conscious being is busy loosening and eroding the foundations below! Through much symptom deadening drug therapy we become acquainted with an **outer** serenity which is as misleading as the calm portrayed by many a flippant actress. The masses rave over her demure manner and pleasing features, only to read at a later date, with staggering horror, that the idol of their life has entered a suicide's grave after years of drug addiction.

Potentially dangerous drugs dished out by an overbusy G.P. are a poor substitute indeed to the fatherly care and concern of the family physician of yesteryears. Nature's warning lights are so often put out of action by a drug industry which subtly conditions chemists, dispensers, and most prominent of all G.Ps by scribble pads and similar gifts used on the average practitioner and dispensers' desk. Yes, and frequently over and above this, grants or conferences in luscious resorts!

In an anti drink and drive society, one might almost feel sympathy for the brewers and distillers when so much is said about the ill effects of alcohol yet hardly a word about dispensed drugs! There must be vast multitudes on our roads who travel around little better than zombies, and that they are doped up to the head and deeply unperturbed about factors that would trigger off a warning response in a normal healthy creature is hardly credit to orthodox medicine. Chemically induced serenity is often fraught with danger, not only for the subject but for society as a whole.

True therapy will rarely make inoperative the symptoms which tell us that something deep down is wrong; it will more often seek to plumb and fathom the cause. It has been truthfully said that no matter how rough the mighty ocean is upon its surface that deep down there is always a great calm; regrettably the reverse is so often the case with man! An outwardly calm and serene surface is often no more than a mask which merely covers up a warring tumult deep down. Even the new art of body language convey's that what one says and what one is, are often poles apart! It is to the depth of our personalities that the true therapist of the mind will chiefly direct treatment. Only as he pursues that policy has he the right to dab the wound on the surface. Much `dis-ease' is the result of an accepted moral dirt having got below the surface. It has been allowed to fester there for years, and though the wound on the surface has been soothed by ointment or liniment, though it be bandaged or even poulticed (I write figuratively) treatment has been most inadequate. The outer wound may appear to have healed but it has merely driven the infection within because it was denied normal outlet. Consequently, the poor victim is beginning to feel a whole host of unpleasant symptoms and these seem to have no connection whatever with a wound that has virtually healed. Yet the patient probably won't even connect the two together and of course what I'm referring to is **not** the body but the mind!

I write as a hypno-analyst, that is, as one who uses hypnosis to accelerate the art of psycho analysis, and not as one who uses hypnosis solely to implant on top of a troubled mind positive suggestions. The reader needs to be aware of this difference in Hypno-therapeutic Practice between Analytical therapy and Suggestion therapy. This is not to decry the valuable work of the latter which the reader will be encouraged to practice on himself in a later chapter. Salve, lotions and liniments do a marvellously successful work; but when festering has occurred deep down and been carried by the blood stream **then** deeper therapy is needed!

The writer has been frequently confronted with clients whose deep neurosis was due to the repression of events which occurred many years previous. And although quite a few of these folk are outwardly serene and seemingly relaxed, therapy, plus the attachment of a bio-feedback monitor, soon unleashes the fact that **inwardly** they are undergoing an unbearable turmoil, and much of their energy has previously been used in keeping the safety valve well and truly down so as to appear **outwardly** composed and respectable. Indeed, the only way to start helping them is to help to lift that valve so as to allow the pressure to diminish. These outwardly respectable upright individuals, **under therapy**, begin to relive events that would under normal disclosure absolutely horrify them. Indeed, so horrific had such events been, when first experienced as growing immature creatures that they repressed them.

Possibly through a restrictive, and often hypocritical standard of morality which could not be reconciled with normal biological vent, these victims not only chose to disavow the experience because of the shame and guilt associated with it, they well and truly, once and for all, blocked the event out of conscious memory; yes, a psychological defence mechanism such as a motorist might undergo in a serious accident, remembering things that preceded and followed the event while the worst part has been repressed with a total amnesia.

But, ah, the mind is not as simple as it outwardly appears! Every single experience undergone since birth is well and truly recorded, and available to be played back again under given circumstances. When the right therapy results in selected playback then that which couldn't be faced once is required to be faced again. What possibility couldn't be faced for shame by a young maturing mind can often be faced later through the maturity and the hindsight of the years. And even though the event must be 're-experienced' - and indeed, the repression has retarded the emotional make up very much to the time in question, - the burden and the trauma can now be shared through rapport with a worthy therapist. In a very real sense a burden then shared becomes indeed a burden halved.

It is the writer's contention that such therapy is not only a truer and nobler alternative therapy to auricular confession in the presence of a cleric, but actually a far more helpful and therapeutic one. There is nothing mechanical about such analysis, nothing judgmental about it; and it is certainly not connected with a Denominational standard of morality chiefly classing virtue with chastity and sin with sex. Yet, having said **that** the writer is convinced that the evangelical cleric appears more suited in some respect to develop such a ministry than many members of other healing professions. This is **not** to disparage the sincerity of others but rather, to affirm that should **they** have discovered or unearthed 'buried guilt' in their client; once they can present it to the patient for the horrible thing it is, they can do little more. They've re-opened an old wound, they've possibly prized open the family cupboard and brought out to view (after possible decades) a dirty skeleton; something the mind had forced out of consciousness and had held down over the decades. But **now** the skeleton in all its filth is open to full view; and the non Christian consultant can merely say, "See it for what it was!"

Alas, this is hardly sufficient for a mind with a standard of morality held high! Conditioning apart, what was sin **then** need not be **less** sinful now! It is because of this possibility that Christian therapists of whom there is thankfully an ever increasing number - can truthfully say, "I've shown you that past act. Because you thought you could just turn over the page and forget it ever occurred I've turned it back for you to face. You see the evil on that page, and though you closed the book and put it in the chest the stench has been coming from that chest down through the years even though you never connected the two."

The suggestion given by a previously dishonest treasurer that his past debts be forgotten, a page be turned over and a new start be commended within the ledger, would hardly be acceptable! In turning over, to commence a new leaf within the ledger, the carry forward column has to be respected. One feels that the same principle rightly applies as much in the moral and spiritual sphere as the economic!

In his far off school days, the present writer well remembers how, after spending several hours on an essay, its completion was marred through a culprit catapulting from his pen a blob of blotting paper soaked in ink which landed on to the neatly finished page creating a frightful mess. Well, in those days teachers were far less lenient than now, so a page or two were turned over very quickly and the same essay was speedily rewritten. Subsequently the few pages deemed necessary for marking were turned back, and after the contents which followed were scanned, top marks were given for that re-written essay. However, near the end of that term marks were then appended or subtracted for overall **past** neatness. The same teacher turned back each page of that exercise book, and when the ruined page was discovered many marks previously given were then deleted because of the appalling mess of that page which I'd sought to conceal by turning over a new leaf. Quite unfair in this instance, as I hadn't been responsible for it in the first place!

Well, many ugly things have occurred in our past lives for which we **are** responsible, and the dictum of turning over a new page and ceasing to cry over spilt milk need not be sufficient in itself. There is a verse in the Old Testament which states, 'God requires that which is past!' Well, one thing **is** sure, our conscience will require it and though we succeed in burying it beneath the surface it still kicks, and subconsciously it lives on even though mentally we may have disavowed its existence.

Past experiences, yes, from those of earliest childhood, are all stored away; and in a very real sense we are the sum of all past experiences many of which we prefer not to know.

The Christian evangelist makes the most of the above situation. He offers a Gospel of eradication for sin, but it is on the condition that we acknowledge our sins and do not seek to cover them up. "I've good news for you;" he says. "A far greater book tells of one who is able to remove all our sins providing we really face, and confess them. (*Proverbs 28:13*). He is able to move them as far away as the east is from the west!" (An immeasurable distance unlike north from south). He tells of One who, though He was sinless, chose to bear the guilt of the sinner and reap the whole penalty for it (*1 Corinthians 15:3*): "His name is Jesus for He shall save His people from their sins!" (*Matthew 1:21*)

The above therapy for the soul as well as the mind can be blest indeed, and the effects wonderfully lasting. Unlike a public and indiscriminate 'laying on of hands' convention for the sick, Christian analytical therapy is specifically suited, as was the healing example of Our Lord, to meet the inner need of each individual. And to any who would doubt such therapy one need only ask, 'which is the easiest to say - Your sins are forgiven you, or Go in Peace for your neurosis is now gone!'

102

CHAPTER XV

SPEAKING TO YOUR OTHER SELF

In the language of Depth Psychology, our consciousness has been compared to the top of an iceberg and our subconscious with the greater part submerged beneath. The latter, although out of conscious knowledge is by far the larger part of our intelligence. Whereas the conscious mind controls factors including eating, drinking, talking, singing and contemplating, the latter includes factors such as those effecting respiration, heartbeat, metabolism and reflex.

Much of what our conscious mind does repetitively will sink out of conscious control to be taken over by the subconscious. For an example, having practised the art of walking, swimming or cycling, you soon cease to have to consciously give it much thought. You just get up and do it while your mind is consciously aware of the direction you're pursuing. And, of course, this is a blessing; for the part of our mind of which we are fully aware (the conscious) rather than being cluttered up with a whole host of factors, it can focus on present and immediate stimuli.

The top mind (the conscious) is critical; and the more alert it is, the more it questions, weighs and assesses. In contrast, the bottom mind (the subconscious) has been termed uncritical: whatever command it receives it normally seeks to actualise. The 'top mind' we might call the executive office on the ground floor where policy is thrashed out and decisions formulated. The 'bottom mind' we might call the workshop in the basement where decisions handed down are unquestioningly transacted; orders are immediately obeyed.

Between the two levels of the mind so briefly and figuratively touched upon, we have what many psychologists have referred to as the end-psychic censor. We might use the analogy of a trapdoor separating the ground floor from the basement and operated by a porter whose duty it is to keep the door shut except when an executive wishes to pass a blueprint down. However, there **are** times when it's possible to put this porter off his guard, and when this has happened an **undesirable** blueprint might well find its way down, there to be transacted. The analogy is, indeed, far from adequate but it helps to explain the kind of method a stage hypnotist may seek to pursue. He knows, through much skill and ingenuity, how best to divert that porter from his task!

A confusing, emotionally fraught atmosphere; subdued lights with expectation, yes, shock tactics that cause the critical faculties to shut down. Such are some of the ways by which that imaginary porter can be stupefied, overtaxed or diverted so that the door into the cellar of the subconscious can be passed through.

Of course, the hypnotic entertainer is not the only operator; what **he** knowingly does has been similarly practised down the centuries by priests or priestesses through the media of religious rituals accompanied with incense, candles and repetitional chants; but without the scientific knowledge of the mechanics involved. Such has resulted in priestly indoctrination, if not brain washing, of the masses; a contrast to Jesus who asked people to weigh and assess before submitting allegiance to Him (*Luke 14:25-33*).

To trust one's mind to another for the reception of positive, noble affirmations can be Divinely transforming; and the need for it is as high amongst Christians as non Christians. Any psychiatric hospital will leave you in no doubt of that! However, as much care should be taken in choosing a doctor, so it should be used in choosing a therapist. Fortunately - with rare exceptions - one is as fully in control of one's actions under hypnosis as out of it. Trilby experiences are purely fiction, and no bona-fide hypnotherapist, to the writer's mind, has ever abused the power of suggestion as have clergy!

Week after week within idyllic hypnotic atmospheres, when to criticize is to sin, these latter encourage their flock to chant either; "We are miserable sinners and there is no health within us" or "pray for us now and at the hour of our death". Need one wonder that on going to Church the faithful appear as going to the dentist; and on leaving appear as having been? One feels like castigating these clerics in black, but I think I can hear One who is much wiser saying; `Father, forgive them - they know not what they do'.

One knows full well that, when the conscious mind is tired or weary then judgement or the critical faculty is much impaired (the porter is being lulled to sleep). A twilight period when the body is relaxed and ready to drift is such an occasion. And, indeed, repetition is always a means of wearing down a critic if for no other reason than to have a bit of peace. Many a mother, of a persistent youngster, knows this to her loss and only too well! Did I not say previously that repetitions can take on the nature of habits which are largely unconscious acts? Such are the factors to be utilized in getting messages passed down from your conscious mind to your subconscious.

The above information, though most inadequate, is of sufficient value for you, dear reader, to know how to pass **constructive** and **positive** affirmations to your other self. This latter will then be working to fulfil at a submerged level what you are putting into practice at the surface; for it is little use suggesting to your conscious self that you are 'the master of every situation' when your subconscious mind has had passed down to it, year after year, that though you try you never seem to succeed. "There I go again!"; "What a silly fool I am!"; "I'm always making a hash of things!". Yes, and **consequently** that's what you become and do!

Wonderful character types are found within the Jewish and Christian scriptures. Two people spring to view as examples of the two levels of the mind (but Oh! there are many more!) - Joseph, the dreamer, and Saul, the first king. The former seemingly dwelt upon dreams of grandeur in the unlikeliest of environments; and though his conscious life was often perplexed with defeat, fortunate for him his subconscious, deep below the surface, was still working to actualise those dreams.

As for the latter character, it would appear that though on the conscious surface everything was put in his favour, deep down within the subconscious depth of his mind he was the victim of insecurity. His outer pride was possibly a camouflage for a constantly held poor self-image deep down. To those interested in such character analysis one might ask: Why did he hold back from informing his uncle of his election for kingship (*1 Samuel 10:16*)? Why, when the big moment came, did he hide amongst the baggage (*Samuel 10:20-23*)? Why did he later reveal a persecution complex (*1 Samuel 22: 6-8*)? And why was he always holding a spear in his hand, even when in the home and eating at the table (*1 Samuel 18:10; 19:9; 20:33; 22:6; and 26:7*)? These were, indeed, expressive of an individual mind consciously intent on making its mark while the subconscious mind, as a fifth columnist, pulled opposite at each attempt. Yes, the mind of so many is divided at differing levels and as troubled as was Rebekah within the womb; two nations are at war within! (*Genesis 25:22 & 23*). A mind, like a city divided against itself (*Matthew 12:25*) cannot stand.

Intense inner conflict within is the cause of neurosis and often leads to a complete breakdown. Two **equally** strong horses attached to a cart, but pulling in opposing directions, results in no progress one way or another. Ultimately, the cart will crack under the strain.

Now you, yourself, may well have consciously desired to be

what, deep down, you or others have conditioned you **not** to be! The previous chapters of this book have been written to re-orientate your consciousness. This chapter is aimed at getting your subconscious to collaborate. Both levels of your mind then pulling in unison, your success is doubly assured.

Admittedly, some folks' symptoms are the effect of powerful unconscious causes deeply buried in the mind but very much alive and active, though out of conscious reach. Irrational fears (i.e. phobias), anxiety attacks and obsessional compulsions are manifestations of such deeply imbedded repressions. In **these** instances the help of a Christian or ethical therapist with bona-fide credentials can be enormous. In the U.S.A. the National Association of Clergy Hypnotherapists is the answer; while in the U.K. we have the International Association of Hypno-Analysts. Both addresses are given at the end of the book. Charismatic deliverance ministries are open to much abuse and mass hysteria, and they carry no indemnity.

I ask that you (to use an Advent collect) "Read, mark, learn and inwardly digest" the pages of this book, and suggest that you also practice some affirmations relevant to your need. As you do, you will, in the words of an old song, actualise the positive and eradicate the negative!

Seven short affirmations:
For overcoming -
Sickness:	'Getting better, Getting better . . . .'
Weakness:	'Strong & healthy, Strong & healthy . .'
Inferiority:	'I'm on top, I'm on top . . . .'
Exam fears:	'I succeed, I succeed . . . .'
Shyness:	'I look at you, I look at you . . . .'
Speech fears:	'Talking better, Talking better . . . .'
Sleeplessness:	'Softly sleeping, Softly sleeping . . . . . .'

Any of the above, apart from the last, could be said silently in time with one's step while out walking. Or to those unafraid of the possibility of drifting into a light self-hypnosis, such wording could be synchronized to the swing and beat of a pendulum when the body is relaxed. The room will need to be subdued, warm and void of draught; and one's feet could be up, tight clothing loosened, and one's eyes allowed to close once they become heavy and weary. Twilight periods are the most suitable and could include not only a siesta during the day but the period before or after the night's sleep.

Committed Christians may choose to derive further benefit by rephrasing their appropriate affirmation in the form of a prayer - **not** of petition but of praise; not for example, 'Lord, make me better!' but rather, 'Thank you, Lord, because you're making me better!' The Master Guru of Christendom said, 'Whatever you ask in prayer, believe that you receive it, **and you will**!' (*Mark 11:24*).

The model affirmations given above are absolutely safe to use within one's home and are merely given as examples. Though they are so simple in style do not for one moment minimise their potential which can sometimes be quite remarkable over even a short period of time. As that most brilliant of all young stage hypnotists, and friend of the writer, Alex LeRoy has said: "Trust me, the simple things in life are usually the best and failure can only occur by trying to complicate them".

A word of warning, however: it is seldom wise to negate pain or fear without first of all enquiring into the cause. Such symptoms are comparable to warning signals on life's railroad. Painful corns are a signal to get proper fitting shoes rather than to persist until one does permanent damage to the feet! A severe migraine may be without physical cause and nothing but good would come from auto-suggestion, but on the contrary it might be the effect of a cerebral tumour; and whereas the power of mind over matter ought **never** to be minimized, 'Professional' advice ought always to be sought first of all from a bona-fide therapist or, indeed, a G.P. Fear also is another

108

factor which usually serves a purpose; it stops us from stepping out in front of the next vehicle; and though it emotively moves me to fight or flee from a tiger it becomes quite meaningless when it makes me scream at a mouse. The former fears are normal and helpful while the latter is irrational and neurotic. We do right to seek relief by self suggestion therapy from the latter but never the former!

In addition to your list of affirmations be sure that they **are** affirmations. One thing that will not register in the subconscious for your success is the negative: 'I am not poorly' is little better than 'I **am**'. The appropriate phrasing should be, 'I am well!'

Another factor, helpful indeed for both levels of the mind, is to have positive affirmations clearly printed on cards where the eyes may constantly fall upon them. These should be put on a bedroom shelf or bedside table where one views them immediately on awakening or last thing before sleeping. They could also be left in a conspicuous position beside a bathroom mirror where one shaves or a dressing table when one prepares. Indeed, the wording might be as follows:

'Action **now!**'
'I'm on top!'
'Today is the first day of the rest of my life!'
'I am the master of all I survey'
'Success is mine!'
'I'm born to conquer!'
'Life is wonderful!'

Specifically spiritual affirmations, often in the form of text cards are commonly found within homes of those whose faith appears to be gloriously radiant rather than gloomily religious. It would appear the precious promises of God's Word had very much sunk into the depth of their subconscious. Like King David they could say, 'Thy word have I hid in my heart that I might not sin against Thee'. None was more human than he, yet none, seemingly, knew the power of assimilated positive affirmations than he did. *(2 Samuel 22: 2-4)* expresses a beautiful chain of them. Why not include them and a whole host of others for your individual need. A Bible concordance will help you to find them; see "Praise and Thanks".

Whatever words or phrases you choose to use, be they secular or spiritual, remember the message of the telegram: it was given prominence because it was urgent; and its wording was short, straight and to the point! Allow any phrases you formulate to be likewise, and the moment they cease to challenge swap them temporarily for another. The wise window dresser keeps changing the display around though the items displayed over the year may be very much the same.

CHAPTER XVI

MUSIC HATH CHARM

Let no one underestimate the hypnotic influence that all music has, and by all I include not only 'hot gospel' hymns and choruses but also peaceful and reverent traditional hymn singing. Some preachers and evangelists are extremely conscious of their effect while others are not. However, the effects are there for all who have eyes to see them.

Indeed, the writer used to delight in switching on the radio to listen to Sunday's half hour of hymn singing. In pre-television years and minus a Radio Times, it was quite a hobby for him and others to guess the Denomination from which the singing was being relayed. More often than not, he and other members of the family guessed right concerning where it came from. If the singing was joyfully melodious and centred round the cross, you were usually on safe ground to affirm it as Methodist. After all, as Wesley himself said: 'Methodism was born in song!' If the service was solemn, dignified and a little starchy, clinically correct but lacking in fervour, it was undoubtedly Anglican! If it were in between and contained psalms in metre, well you knew it to be Presbyterian or Congregationalist. If the singing were accompanied on a grand piano and expressed joy but lightness then it would most probably be from some evangelical centre. And if it were peppered and salted with Amens and Hallelu-jahs - with band instead of an organ - you couldn't go wrong; it was most certainly Salvation Army.

It is equally true to say that not only the kind of service but primarily the music that accompanies it has quite a lasting effect on those who've attended. The countenance of those leaving a high mass or a choral eucharist carry a differing countenance from those leaving a Methodist, Nazarene or Pentecostal service. Those leaving a Brethren or Free Kirk will also reflect a differing brand of inner glow. Remember, however, that solemnity is not **always** a bad thing, and a cheesy smile is not necessarily proof of a **deep** spiritual fervour. It is frequently no more than cosmetic.

It is regrettable to find that certain evangelists renowned for four square healing rallies - while publicly denouncing hypnotic techniques as diabolic are blatantly following them to a fine art. I have recently witnessed, first hand, a charismatic healer using a psychological confusion trick on those who'd come forward for either salvation or the laying on of hands 'with signs following'. That he hadn't known he was doing it is very difficult to accept. Indeed, the likeness of some charismatic rallies to a stage hypnotists show has to be seen to be believed. Flaking out and falling back 'in the spirit' is frequently effected in as identical a fashion as that used by any stage hypnotist. The repetition of highly charged chorus singing, which frequently accompanies these healing rallies is frequently done for a specific effect. The worshippers are swayed into a state of wakeful hypnosis and once 'completely out' suggestions of healing are imparted. They are then, frequently, conditioned into affirming a cure. And when such a positive response follows it is accompanied by adulation towards them, and, of course, further singing - we trust - 'to the glory of Jesus'.

The writer wishes to affirm that he is by no means opposed to all forms of praise and healing which go under the term charismatic. Though he, personally, much prefers the method Jesus commonly used Himself (*Luke 5:14 & 8:56*), there are, nevertheless, occasions when (to use a Jesuit saying) 'The end justifies the means'. I think Paul knew it! (*Philippians 1:18*). The hypocrisy is surely with those evangelists who denounce a psychological process, yet blatantly utilize it themselves.

If bodies can occasionally be healed through Four Square healing rallies, and the glory given to the Saviour, the method used is of lesser importance than the end product: a body healed! Similarly, that many people have been wooed forward to make their spiritual commitment, through the gentle playing of 'Just as I am' at a Billy Graham rally, is a blessing indeed. If such a 'back up' has resulted in more people surrendering their lives to Jesus, who but a Christian bigot will disparage such a 'back up'! The difference surely, is that Billy Graham has openly acknowledged, more than once, the valuable part that hypnosis can play both medically and day to day within peoples' lives. Whereas a few in excitable Deliverance ministries, in common with the less excitable Christian Scientists and Seventh Day Adventists, have branded such a usage as satanic. One very much feels it's a case of the frying pan having called the kettle black!

Soft light, conducive architecture, warm atmospheres, and music to influence the emotions to which suggestive words are given, have all a legitimate part to play in back up for proclaiming the Word of God which is a living force and the power of God unto salvation to all who accept it (*Romans 1:16*). However, all such aids should be no more than 'back up', otherwise the converts will not last long and neither might their healing. And as for any who may feel disposed to discarding 'back up', let them be consistent, and rejecting all external emotional appeal, simply read The Word without external interference. They will need to worship in a fashion comparable to the early Quakers. A contrast to the emotively charged periods of Christian Revival! Quakerism, with high philanthropic ideals, has **not** evolved along fundamentalist based guide lines. Its heart is too all embracing for that. The Spirit of Christ comes before the 'letter of the law'. (*II Corinthians 3:6*)

113

In daily activity, whether it be switching on radio or TV, entering a Christian or New Age book shop or witnessing a band: Salvationist or secular, music will sway us one way or another. Only the retarded or gullible will underestimate its influence. If you want confirmation, just look into the pupils of those who are listening! While Wagner's "Tannhauser" will stir up one type of emotion and Ravel's "Balero" another, Brahm's "Lullaby" will create yet another. Though we might like to think otherwise we are all victims swayed by emotive forces throughout each day, and music is such an emotive force for good or bad.

Concerning the latter, the leaders of the Third Reich knew, full well, that music has charms and they didn't hesitate to use it to the full. "Deutschland über alles", accompanied with feet marching in goose step formation, could not only spur on the Nazis hopefully to victory; it could not only put fear in the enemy; it could, in fact, so thrill the opposition, because of the emotive fervour the music created, that they might be subconsciously swayed towards secretly supporting them instead!

Indeed, when the Austrian national anthem was sung in those far off war years the writer, familiar with such a hymn tune, felt that Hitler could never have been the evil character that the British were seeking to paint him; and he was far from being alone in entertaining such an opinion: How could the one who loved such beautiful, soul inspiring, music be the one responsible for those news reel flashes of Nazi atrocities. It appeared as if the latter was no more than false propaganda from the British War Department.

The writer, during past decades, has occasionally visited healing shrines such as Walsingham in Norfolk and the shrine of St. Winifride in North Wales. Indeed, concerning the latter, when not only a presumed part of the cross of Jesus was brought out for veneration, but also a finger of the dead St. Winifride, the atmosphere was so charged by children singing an emotive hymn that tears

114

welled up. It proved intensely hard to believe (even though brought up a staunch Protestant) that, in such an atmosphere, one was practising idolatry. Was it **really** all that wrong to worship the Madonna when such beautiful hymn singing was associated with her life like image! Yes, as in political regimes, so similarly in religious regimes throughout the world, the emotive use of music can sway if not distort completely one's better judgement.

As youngsters, who amongst us didn't feel a thrill down the spine when listening to a brass band! Who, amongst young men listening to Susa's "Liberty Bell" did not imagine marching with others round a quarter deck! Who in Scotland does not want to tap dance in time with a fiddle orchestra playing! or who amongst the ladies hasn't wanted to do a Highland dance when an appropriate tunes comes on! Yes, all are agreed that appropriate music can get one's feet moving. then why shouldn't it be utilised with appropriate words to get our feet moving for the Gospel of Christ? (I'm speaking here specifically to believers. I ask others to bear with me.)

William Booth realised the power of such a force as music. He took over many of the Devil's best tunes and attached spiritually suggestive words to them. And since his day many other evangelists have done likewise. Indeed, one of the most thrilling experiences witnessed by the writer was during Sundays in the late nineteen forties. As a teenager in Newcastle on a Sunday afternoon, the traffic would make way for the Salvation Army marching down a busy thoroughfare on its way to the Westgate Citadel. It was extremely difficult holding back tears of gratitude, as one witnessed the flag flying for Jesus, the Salvationists walking in dignified array, and most of all a brass band playing to the glory of one's risen and glorified Lord. If ever music had charms, believe me it did on those occasions when one's faith was still so new.

Life, being as hectic as it is, we often have little opportunity to get away from the hustle and bustle in order to rest for awhile.

However, to enter a place of solitude in order to momentarily rest is helpful. And if it is accompanied by appropriate music, it becomes more helpful still. Indeed, the last place of worship to which the writer was Rector, frequently provided restful music in the background. Either such music was purely restful and unassociated with words, or else it conjured up verses associated with the Saviour. And what was started as an experiment became regular due to much public demand.

As human beings we are not robots or daleks but, creatures of much emotion - and the Church has frequently got so involved in doctrine and dogma as to neglect the emotive needs of the heart. What ever abuses the charismatic movement may be guilty of, thank God, it has never been guilty of ignoring the emotive yearnings of the heart. To that extent it has much to teach us. Love comes from the heart whereas legalism comes from the head!

We do well to benefit from God's gift of music. King Saul benefitted from the harp of young David (*1 Samuel 16:23*). When spirits of depression engulf us we do well to resort to it. The psalmist exhorts the people of God to sing no less than 67 times. Then let us sing words of optimism,. assurance and gratitude, and if we wed them to tunes that speak to another level of our mind then the effect may, indeed be quite 'tranceforming' to ourselves and, what is more, the greater glory of God.

Living as a cleric can be quite an isolated experience. One should hardly pick out certain parishioners with whom to form a close attachment. Favouritism expressed by clergy is a harmful thing within any parish set up. Consequently, Christian books, plus audio tapes, can be a boon for any Christian worker. In giving out spiritually one feels that virtue has gone out (*Luke 6:19 & 8:46*). But how to replenish that spiritual void is a task confronting every Christian worker. For those unable to attend conventions, conferences and seminars, nothing can be more rewarding than a stock of spiritual books **plus** a selection of spiritual cassettes!

Throughout the day, having sought God's guidance as to whom next to visit - on the car journey from one place to the next - the playing of Christian music on one's car cassette player, can be tremendously beneficial. During the war years and after, Music While You Work spurred on people to make munitions. If you are a committed Christian then you too will realise that you are at war - at war with the army of Satan. Take it from me, the sound of spiritual songs will likewise spur **you** on to make those spiritual munitions to combat all the fiery darts of your adversary!

The apostle Paul admonishes the Christian to sing, making melody in his heart to the Lord (*Ephesians 5:19*). The believer needs this daily booster, and it can become very real through the medium of a car cassette player, as indeed it later can through a music centre by your warm fire side in the evening.

Near the end of the day, either laid out on a rug or else relaxed in a comfortable chair, with lights subdued and draughts excluded, what bliss it can be to switch on a record or a cassette and listen to the sound of soft, relaxing, slumberland music. For the good of your health, and the benefit of others around you, you need to practice such a stress management procedure. It's so simple and yet the results, if routinely adhered to, can be quite out of this world. Don't discard it because of its simplicity. And for those who have made a personal commitment to Christ, there is the added advantage of not only listening to music that relaxes the mind and, through it, the body: there is the added blessing of words being appended to music - which tell of the change that has been wrought since Jesus was, simply, invited into one's heart to save one's soul.

The Cliff Richards', John Cash's and Helen Shapiro's had, in their heyday all the adulation this world could give them. yet they felt a void in their lives. it seemed as if they were living on two dimensions when God wanted them to run on three. Thankfully, although in publicly deciding to hand over the reigns of their lives to Jesus, they appeared to have everything to lose and possibly nothing to gain, they still took the simple step of faith. They asked Jesus to come into their lives. Having done it they were not ashamed to testify to what they had done. And you must know dear reader, as well as I, that they've never had cause to look back since. Indeed, countless other musicians and singers, down the centuries have done the same, and their temperaments have been as diverse and varied as a George Handel from a George Hamilton!

The God of the Christian is **not** a disappointment to those who've taken the simple step of inviting Him into their hearts and then confessed Him before others as their new found Lord and Master (*Romans 10:9*). Too many have discarded the grand old Gospel because it appears too simple to work (*John 6:29*). Like Naaman in the Old Testament, if told to do something difficult they respond; when told to do something extremely simple they hesitate (*2 Kings 5:13*). How would Naaman have fared if he'd just kept on procrastinating!

Quite a spiritual rejuvenation took place in the life of the present writer during his last `living'. This came about largely through video tapes of the Ulster evangelist Derick Bingham **and** through the inspired hymn singing which accompanied the same. But then, is not this quite normal? Hymn singing has been as much a part of any Spiritual Awakening as has a preaching ministry. Hymns to delightfully emotive tunes, linked to words centred round the Cross of Jesus, have touched the heart and moved multitudes. And, has not history shown that the deeper the experience, the deeper become the words and the more heart provoking the music that accompanies it!

The hymns that never grow old, like the Gospel they proclaim - together with the tunes compiled and wedded to them - reflect the spiritual depth of those who first sang them.

Reader, if your head is singing in the heavens make sure your feet are firmly grounded on the rock (*1 Corinthians 3:11*). May your emotions never sway you from the one and only way to success. May they be your aids but never your compass. Let emotional impetus only be harnessed to the path you know to be right. Many think they know the path but are quite mistaken (*Proverbs 14:12*). Be sure you are on it, (*John 14:6*), travelling in the right direction, and **then** why not confirm it with a song!

CHAPTER XVII

AND NOW TO ACTION

Well now, much time has been taken I trust in assimilating the contents of these pages. This is most necessary. However, unless you start putting what you are learning into action, then it will avail you little. There is an old, wise saying: 'An ounce of practice is worth a ton of theory'. Indeed, your dreams unexpressed by deeds are but the assimilation of attention and emotion, generated but then denied an outlet. Through attention and visualisation, one's emotions become active. And the purpose of emotion is primarily to give impetus and driving force to the will of man. It is obvious, therefore, that if you direct the stream towards a dam which refuses it outlet, then you are courting disaster. The dykes will either burst their banks or else the water will spill over and create havoc, seeping through into forbidden areas. Because of such factors, it is, therefore, always unwise to generate emotion that cannot be ultimately given vent through constructive action. One usually revs up an engine to make a speedy getaway. If one repeatedly does so when the clutch is disengaged, then the engine is soon likely to be damaged and will not last long. These analogies are well worth bearing in mind.

Folk almost void of emotion may be far from desirable characters to meet. But their opposites, folk who grovel in sentiment and emotion while refusing to act, are even worse. Such sickly, spineless creatures are reminiscent of that Victorian temperament which wallowed in sentiment over a music hall melodrama, yet was unmoved to action concerning the poverty that encircled it. People who judged the success of a play by the amount of tears it could produce, and yet were unmoved by the plight of the urchins and women of the streets outside, were in a state of mind which was not only psychologically sick, but was morally repugnant!

A previous chapter emphasised the need of having vision and a goal as an objective. The Good Book says, and rightly so, 'Without vision the people perish'. (*Proverbs 29:18*). We need to have that vision which will not only benefit ourselves, but through so doing - by our newfound optimism and joy - make us more helpful and congenial towards all creatures with whom we share this planet. Yes, the effect must always be that we 'Do great deeds, and don't just dream them!' Dreams **can** be used as a substitute for deeds; and this was previously touched on, see it never happens with you! So many dear souls have found the outside world so unbearably harsh and cruel that they largely create a make-believe world as a substitute for a live world. They have withdrawn from fact into fiction. And once the thin line of demarcation between fantasy and reality has been broken, they have gone psychotic with a one way ticket! After all, why should a person seek release from a world of such compensations? Those in the worst wards of mental institutions are often content with their lot: they can be kings and queens in a world now more real to them (alas, to no one else) than their heartbreaking previous existence. The latter was so unbearable that it has been buried for all time.

Your need is now to fuel the desires, dreams and deeds of your mind with the contemplation of success. Have not only visions of bouncing through life with vim, vigour and vitality but, equally, an attitude which uses every bounce as a bounce forward.

We've discussed 'doing and not just dreaming'. "That's all very well," you may say; "But how do I start?" The answer is that you see your role as a creature of action. 'Procrastination is the thief of time.' 'He who hesitates is lost.' 'Put not off till tomorrow what you can do today.' Such sayings are common to our vocabulary, and they were concocted by those who had learned through the oldest and wisest of all places of learning: 'the school of hard knocks', which has also been touched upon. It is, temporarily, easier to put off a difficult task than to face it. But be assured that from a long term viewpoint, it is always disastrous. Remember, to play the coward and run away from the bully may give temporary relief, but it merely gives more power to the opponent, and for him, too, success breeds success.

However, often the crudest of creatures can be largely trained to become a trifle more amiable. It's a matter of rewarding good conduct by attention and opposing bad by rejection.

One point you must expect, indeed anticipate. When you start acting in a different way from that in which you've acted throughout most of your previous life, you'll feel for a while strange and also uneasy. It's much more comfortable, as a rule, to wear the old shoes that let the rain in than to wear a new pair which keep the rain out! The 'breaking in' process is equally a trifle painful, whether it be a pair of shoes for the feet or a horse for transport. Newness is also as strange when one takes full control of the reins of his or her life for the first time. It will be every bit as strange as was mounting a bike, or swimming in the sea! New experiences are often far from pleasant, but practice makes perfect when persisted in: the end goal is worth the bumps or duckings occasionally encountered on the way. You know that all this is so: then start bouncing with radiance through life **from now.**

Some might think, 'What's got over her?' 'Why does he act differently?' 'Who does she think she is?' Well, as touched on, let them think as they may. You persist, and eventually they will usually come round to putting the same value upon you as you actually put upon yourself! Remember, 'As a person thinketh in his heart, so is he'.

Need I emphasise again that if you are a practising Christian you refrain from false humility? You are of more value than the many sparrows over each of which your Maker is concerned. Yes, even the fifth one that was 'thrown in' for good measure! (*Matthew 10:29 and Luke 12:6*). The Saviour died for you; you are of value to God! Whatever your religious persuasion should happen to be, if it teaches you to grovel and become a doormat, then you would be very wise to question its validity.

A final question! "When are you going to start doing what you have been dreaming? Acting out what you are anticipating?" The hardest thing of all is often to make the first move. In far-off days, it was a frequent experience to perceive a fellow in a shunting yard by a busy station, walking with pressure against a train of coaches or trucks, keeping them moving by his own sole effort. The fact was simply this; the momentum that only a shunting engine could start, a solitary railway employee could continue. Well, once you have started a line of action, believe me, you will find it comparatively easy to keep it going. Start a new momentum of assertiveness in your character and what follows will become in comparison, easy to continue.

"Ah", you reply, "that analogy you gave is just not good enough. What I need in my life is not only the power of an original push comparable to that from a shunting engine, but the ability to keep up that momentum for the rest of my days! From where could I possibly receive such a perpetual driving force?" Well, I have good news for you via a complementary analogy: we move away from the old-time shunting yard adjacent to many a station to a delightful sea-scene adjacent to a harbour of yesteryear. Here, heading out towards the horizon, one schooner is moving one way while another, moved by the same wind, is moving in the opposite direction.

'One ship sails east and one sails west, while the selfsame breezes blow.
*'Tis **not** the gales but the set of the sails that decides the way they go!'*

123

Though a host of advice has been given to you in the preceding chapters, most of it can never be implemented unless you are faced with the obstacles touched upon. The bullies, the previously assumed setbacks, stumbling blocks and opponents of your plans, are nothing less than the gales which drive the yacht of your life one way or several! For where there is no such force, believe me, the stillness will result in a stationary situation which results in utter stagnation. Your life, void of continual gales, has hardly the ability to surmount the waves. It would simply drift.

Concerning drifting with the gales, the writer recalls well such a life! A man of mettle fought and strove against many odds in order to establish a lucrative business. His only son was shielded by his mother against every storm imaginable. The years passed by and the business was passed down from father to son. Regrettably, what the father had taken almost a lifetime to achieve, the son demolished within five years. No gales had ever been encountered by the heir until the business had irretrievably stagnated. When they did, he proved totally incapable. Yet he was not to blame; his parents had actually 'choked him with cream!'

Reader and friend, the gales of life are essential to all of us; and if our sails are set correctly, the more of them we experience the swifter we'll make headway. Of course, observing things superficially, to drift **with** the gale seems the easier route because it is the path of no resistance. Indeed, for this very reason it is the way pursued by the fibreless, the morally spineless, the jellyfish of society! However, speedily drifting gets folk nowhere because it leads to a change in course as often as a change in the wind's direction. Those who follow such a philosophy are to be met with each day. As often as their environment changes so does their attitude. With with the gang in the factory, office, or local, their moral outlook and form of expression is so contrary to when they are at home that one wonders whether or not they are moral schizophrenics. The simple fact is that every environment they enter begins to mould them into its pattern temporarily. One thing is obvious, they prove powerless to mould it.

Dear friends, with your newly acquired knowledge - through the assimilation of these pages - you are now truly able to set your sails appropriately, not to drift with the gales but, by their aid, to tack into them for the purpose of surmounting them. You can, from this moment onwards, thank your Maker for each gale that blows in your direction, for, as I say, it becomes nothing less than the very driving force required to move you speedily forward. Each of life's gales, for those with properly adjusted sails, becomes not only that primary shove, but also the perpetual momentum for each of life's noble pursuits and aspirations. These gales are forces which are as essential, to those who wish to progress morally and spiritually, as petrol is to a car, diesel is to a coach, or electricity is to a tram. Is it any wonder that the Apostle James could say to the saints of his day, "Consider it pure joy, my brothers, when you face trials of many kinds." (*James 1:2*).

Is it any wonder that the greatest guru for all western civilisation could say, "Blessed are you when people insult you, persecute you and falsely say all kinds of evil against you because of me." (*Matthew 5:11*).

The greater the gales the more glorious can the character become. Remember the words of Browning:

'Life's just the stuff to try the soul
Educe the man!'

Now, obviously, you would hardly be wise to secure the position of helmsman on a schooner if you're incompetent to control the tiller of a yacht! You would hardly become a diver if you were not already an elementary swimmer! You do not- if you're sensible - mount a 500cc motorbike before you've mastered the knack of riding a pedal cycle! The wise individual starts with the mastering of small tasks, and as success leads to success, so he moves on to master more advanced and heavier ones.

In a similar way, start mastering small grievances. Assert yourself, and experience the joy of victory over these. Then move on to the next rung of the ladder and use a similar strategy. Do not rest until you've got to the top! Your goal is nothing less than the top rung; nevertheless, only an accident-prone fool ignores those rungs between. Try each step as you reach it and then stamp your foot forcefully upon it as you ascend to make contact with the next.

The Chinese have, amongst their ancient lore, a saying relevant to our task in view: 'A journey of a thousand miles begins with the first step.' Indeed it does. One might buy a ticket from Aberdeen to London, enter the appropriate platform and know that the train waiting there will take one to the required destination. But unless one steps aboard, the cost involved and the knowledge gained will have been of no avail.

To take the vital step is to **act** upon what one believes. You have the knowledge at your fingertips with which to radiantly 'bounce' through life with vim, vigour and vitality. The cost has involved your valuable time in digesting this book. If you have acted upon it fully, you will not only be gloriously set up for time but for eternity too.

Friend, this is the first day of the rest of your life. It's **never** too late to begin. Then start acting upon it today.

- END -

There are many ethical hypnotherapy associations providing lists of bona fide therapists (stamped addressed envelope appreciated!) The author can personally commend the following:

Neil French's INTERNATIONAL ASSOCIATION OF HYPNO-ANALYSTS, P.O.Box 180, Bournemouth, BH3 7YR UK

Bill Curtis's NATIONAL ASSOCIATION OF CLERGY HYPNOTHERAPISTS, 501, Maynard Avenue, Florence, South Carolina, 29505, USA.

Frank Lennon's NATIONAL REGISTER OF ADVANCED HYPNOTHERAPISTS, P.O.Box 318, Wembley, Middlesex HA9 6AE UK

Otherwise, feel free to contact the author of this book via: Ty Coch Publishing, Fron Park Road, Holywell, Flintshire CH8 7UY UK.

1.